A History of
AIRSHIPS

A History of

AIRSHIPS

John Richards

First published 2009

The History Press
The Mill, Brimscombe Port
Stroud, Gloucestershire, GL5 2QG
www.thehistorypress.co.uk

British Library Cataloguing in Publication Data.
A catalogue record for this book is available from the British Library.

ISBN 978 0 7524 4536 6

Printed in Great Britain

CONTENTS

ILLUSTRATIONS

INTRODUCTION

An airship is a lighter-than-air craft which is dirigible – it can be steered and ascending and descending can be done in a controlled manner. Balloons are always at the mercy of the wind, and from the first man-carrying flights a search began for some effective means of control. As Dr Johnson observed in 1784 'The vehicles are no use until we can steer them.' This could not be done until a balloon could be driven by a source of power other than the wind: man-power (rowing and pedalling) was tried, and steam. But real progress began with the introduction of the electric motor and the petrol engine.

This book begins with a brief account of some of the attempts to invent an effective dirigible balloon, and then moves on to the early airships which appeared from the 1880s up to the start of the First World War in 1914. During that war airships were used for reconnaissance and bombing – most intensively in the German raids on Britain.

Between the two world wars was the era of huge civil airships such as the German *Graf Zeppelin* and *Hindenburg* and the British *R100* and *R101*. In the same period the United States commissioned the large naval airships *Los Angeles*, *Shenandoah*, *Akron* and *Macon*. During the Second World War the United States Navy deployed the largest airship fleet ever. Post-war, small blimps have been used for advertising and surveillance.

This book deals with its subject in a non-technical way, but some basic information will be found useful:

Size – It is worth knowing the dimensions of an airship so that comparisons may be made with other craft. The usual measurements given are length and maximum diameter.

Capacity – An airship is able to rise because of the use of a gas which is lighter than the surrounding air; hydrogen was used for many years, then helium. The gas either fills the whole envelope or is contained in bags or cells within the envelope. The capacity of the lifting gas containers is given in cubic feet.

Some examples of airship dimensions and capacities will illustrate their comparative sizes:

1884 *La France:* 165ft long x 27ft maximum diameter. Capacity: 66,000 cubic feet.
1902 *Spencer:* 93ft long x 24ft diameter. Capacity: 30,000 cubic feet.
1904 *California Arrow:* 52ft long x 17ft diameter. Capacity: 8,000 cubic feet.
1929 *R100:* 709ft long x 133ft diameter. Capacity: 5,000,000 cubic feet.
1931 *Akron:* 758ft x 133ft diameter. Capacity: 6,500,000 cubic feet.
1936 *Hindenburg:* 800ft long x 135ft diameter. Capacity: 7,500,000 cubic feet.

The Spencer airship was about six times longer than today's average family car; the *Akron* and the *Hindenburg* were both more than twice as long as a soccer field, and three times as long as a Boeing 747 aircraft .

The approach taken in this book is to focus on developments within individual countries. To give an overall view an *Airship Timeline* is provided, highlighting significant events in the history of dirigibles, and the books and articles listed in the bibliography are recommended for further reading.

ILLUSTRATION CREDITS

The Dock Museum, Barrow-in-Furness: 33.
Cardiff Libraries: 26, 27.
Library of Congress: 1, 2, 5, 7, 32, 36, 41, 42, 43, 77.
Mirror Syndication International: 71, 72.
Royal Aeronautical Society Library: 21, 22, 49, 51, 52, 54.
Courtesy of the Bruce/Leslie Collection, licensor www.scran.ac.uk: 47, 48.
Zeppelin Luftschifftechnik: 84.

I

THE PIONEERS

FRANCE

THE MONTGOLFIER BROTHERS

Forty-three years old Joseph-Michel Montgolfier and his younger brother Jacques Étienne, sons of a paper manufacturer, had completed private trials of their new device and were ready for a public demonstration. Their hot-air balloon ascended on 4 June 1783, at Annonay, about forty miles south of Lyon.

The balloon was 35ft in diameter, made of three thicknesses of paper and linen. Underneath was a brazier, burning straw and wool. The heated air rose into the envelope, the unmanned balloon ascended, and travelled one and a half miles before coming to earth, whereupon it caught fire. News of the Montgolfiers' success was sent to the Academy of Sciences in Paris, which set up a commission to look into possible future developments in flight. After interviewing Jacques Étienne Montgolfier the members of the commission decided to subsidise further work, and arranged to show off the invention to Louis XVI. The demonstration took place at Versailles on 19 September 1783, using a new balloon. The flight lasted for under ten minutes, covering two miles, and carried a cockerel, a duck and a sheep, which all came through their ordeal unscathed.

The first man-carrying flight, which lasted for about twenty minutes, took place on 21 November 1783, when the Mongolfier balloon – 70ft high and 46ft in diameter – took up Jean-Francois Pilâtre de Rozier and Francois Laurent, the marquis d'Arlandes. The ascent was made from the Chateau de la Muette, in the Bois de Boulogne, in the presence of official observers, including Benjamin Franklin, ambassador of the United States.

The balloon, bigger than the one which had ascended at Versailles, carried the two aeronauts in a wicker gondola and to keep the balloon aloft they had to keep adding straw to the fire in the brazier. Franklin wrote that:

> This method of filling the balloon with hot air is cheap and expeditious, and it is supposed may be sufficient for certain purposes, such as elevating an engineer to take a view of an enemy's army, works, &c., conveying intelligence into or out of a besieged town, giving signals to distant places, or the like.

JACQUES ALEXANDRE CÉSAR CHARLES (1746–1823)

After starting his career in finance, Charles became interested in experimental physics when he was about thirty-five. His balloon was much smaller than that of the Montgolfier brothers' and was filled with hydrogen, which was made by pouring sulphuric acid over iron filings. (Henry Cavendish had produced hydrogen in this manner in 1766, calling it 'inflammable gas',

1 J.A.C. Charles and Nicolas Robert making the first flight in a hydrogen balloon, in front of the Palais des Tuileries, on 1 December 1783.

and found it to be lighter than common air). On 26 August 1783 the unmanned balloon rose from the Champ de Mars in Paris, coming to earth twelve miles away, when it was destroyed by apprehensive peasants, who thus set a trend which was to be a feature of several early flights. Benjamin Franklin described the craft to Sir Joseph Banks:

> The balloon is only 26ft diameter being filled with air ten times lighter than common air, will carry up a greater weight than the other (the Montgolfiers'), which though vastly bigger was filled with an air that could scarcely be more than twice as light … These machines must always be subject to being driven by winds. Perhaps mechanic art may find easy means to give them progressive motion in calm, and to slant them a little towards the wind.

Ten days after the Montgolfier manned ascent, on 1 December 1783, the Tuileries were crowded with paying spectators when J.A.C. Charles and Nicolas Robert ascended in their hydrogen-filled balloon to 1,800ft and flew for twenty-five miles.

The commission of the Academy of Sciences met to receive reports on the flights of the two kinds of balloons – the Montgolfière and the Charlière – and to consider their future. There was certainly intense public interest, and balloon flights for many years to come were to attract crowds of spectators. But the commission agreed with Franklin that it was essential to seek some means of steering the craft. In October 1784, in England, Dr Samuel Johnson wrote to a friend: 'We now know a method of mounting into the air, and, I think, are not likely to know more. The vehicles can serve no use till we can guide them.'

It would take over a hundred years to achieve such a balloon.

JEAN-BAPTISTE MEUSNIER (1754–93)

Meusnier, a mathematician and engineer in the French Army, presented plans for a dirigible to the Academy of Sciences in 1784. Instead of the spherical balloon, Meusnier's design envisaged an envelope in the form of an ellipse (with horizontal fins to provide stability) to which was attached a boat-shaped gondola. He proposed that there should be three propellers, rotated by a system of ropes and pulleys. After Meusnier had calculated that eighty men would be needed to crank the propellers, he concluded that his design would be impracticable. Nevertheless, it was Meusnier who pointed the way towards an aerodynamically feasible shape for airships.

Meusnier also invented the *ballonet*. It was found that gas used for lifting a balloon was liable to leak, and in any case it expands or contracts with changes in atmospheric pressure (as when ascending or descending) and temperature. These changes in the volume of the gas made it impossible to maintain a balloon's shape. Meusnier's solution to this problem was to install a bag inside the balloon – common air was introduced into this bag by means of a pump or blower and released through a valve. As the lifting gas contracts, more air goes into the ballonet; as the gas expands, air is removed from the ballonet and released into the atmosphere. The pressure on the envelope thus remains constant and the balloon keeps its shape. Meusnier's invention is still in use today.

JEAN-PIERRE FRANCOIS BLANCHARD (1753–1809)

One of those who attempted to achieve more control over a balloon was Jean-Pierre Blanchard, born in 1753 at Les Andelys, Normandy. His balloon flew from the Champ de Mars in Paris on 2 March 1784, and had paddles operated by a man-powered treadle. He was in the air for about one-and-a-quarter hours, travelling just over a mile. The hydrogen was made using a circle of ten barrels containing sheet iron, rather than iron filings.

On 7 January 1785 Blanchard and the American Dr John Jeffries made the first flight across the Channel, from Dover to Calais. They carried oars, nine bags of ballast and 'a large inflated bladder, containing a number of letters from people of the first distinction in this country to several of the French nobility; a compass and some philosophical instruments, a small bottle of brandy, two beautiful silk ensigns, English and French; a few biscuits, and two cork jackets.' (*The Times*, 11 January 1785).

Over the next four years Blanchard made ascents in several European countries, and demonstrated his parachute, dropping a cat from a balloon before using the apparatus himself when he had to escape from a damaged balloon. (The early parachutes were like umbrellas with wooden frames. The first recorded descent with such a device was made on Boxing Day, 1783, when Louis-Sébastien Lenormand jumped from the tower of the observatory at Montpellier. André Jacques Garnerin was the first to use a frameless parachute, dropping from a balloon over Parc Monceau in Paris on 22 October 1797. Garnerin's wife, Jeanne-Geneviève, became the first female parachutist).

With his wife, Marie – the first woman to fly alone in a balloon – Blanchard made the first balloon flights in Belgium, Germany, the Netherlands, Poland and the United States. He died at The Hague on 7 March 1808, having made a total of about sixty balloon ascents, and may be regarded as the first professional aviator.

FRENCH MILITARY BALLOONING

It was envisaged from the beginning that lighter-than-air craft could be used for military purposes. The first in army employment was the *L'Entreprenant*, built in 1793 at the Chateau de Chalais-Meudon, near Paris, under the direction of Charles Coutelle. In the following year the tethered balloon was deployed at Maubeuge, which was under siege, and the airborne observers found that they were able to report on Dutch and Austrian troop movements and positions. The Austrians tried to shoot the balloon down, and complained that its use contravened the laws of war. (As George Orwell was to write 150 years later: 'Every weapon seems unfair until you have adopted it yourself.')

The battle of Fleurus, on 26 June 1794, lasted for about ten hours, with the observation balloon in the air for the whole time. By 1796 the French Army had four balloon units, operating *L'Entreprenant*, *Céleste*, *Hercule* and *Intrépide*, but three years later Napoleon closed down the balloon operations and the Meudon workshop.

Military balloons were next employed by the French in the Franco-Prussian War of 1870–71. Paris was besieged but communications were maintained by balloon: on 23 September 1870 the first left Paris, with mail, and flew for fifty-six miles. By the end of the siege, in January 1871, sixty-six flights had been made, carrying mail and 368 carrier-pigeons which were supposed to bring back messages. Only fifty-seven returned.

There was still no means of controlling or guiding flights – one balloon ended up in Norway.

GASPARD FÉLIX TOURNACHON (NADAR) (1820-1910)

'Nadar' was an artist – he drew caricatures, and became the most famous French photographer of his day – and also a balloonist. His *Le Géant* was the largest balloon yet: 212,000 cubic feet long and 197ft high. The gondola, 13ft x 8ft, had a captain's cabin, a lavatory, a storeroom and a photographic darkroom. The flight of 18/19 October 1863 was an ordeal – after sixteen hours in the air the balloon was hit by a storm, which dragged *Le Géant* across the face of the earth at about 30mph, narrowly missing a railway train, and smashing down trees and telegraph poles. People and equipment fell out and were left scattered along the ground. All were injured, but alive. *Le Géant* finally came to a halt near Hannover.

STANISLAS CHARLES HENRI DUPUY DE LÔME (1816–85)

Dupuy de Lôme, a graduate of the École Polytechnique, became famous as a naval architect. During the siege of Paris the government supported his attempt to develop a dirigible balloon, work which he later carried on at his own expense. It made its only flight on 2 February 1872, from the fort at Vincennes, with fourteen on board, including eight sailors – four at a time cranked the propeller. The balloon, which had a rudder and a ballonet, covered ninety miles in about two hours.

ALBERT TISSANDIER (1839–1906) AND GASTON TISSANDIER (1843–99)

The brothers Tissandier flew in balloons out of the besieged city of Paris in the autumn of 1870. Albert was an architect, archaeologist, writer and illustrator. Gaston a scientist and author. On 15 April 1875 Gaston Tissandier, Joseph Crocé-Spinelli and Henri Theodore Sivel, in the balloon *Zénith* (106,000 cubic feet) tried to break the altitude record of Coxwell and Glaisher, and attained a height of over 26,000ft. Gaston Tissandier passed out several times, and his two companions died. They are commemorated by a monument at the Père Lachaise cemetery. Gaston and Albert Tissandier were later to build the first airship to be powered by an electric motor.

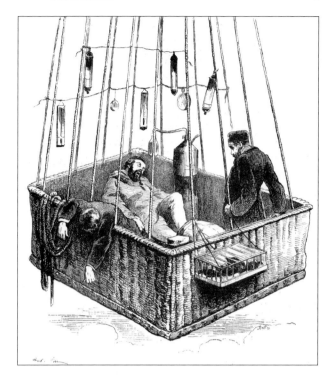

2 Henri Sivel, Joseph Crocé-Spinelli and Gaston Tissandier in the basket of the balloon *Zénith*. They ascended to over 26,000ft, but Sivel and Crocé-Spinelli died. Gaston Tissandier became unconscious, but survived. He was later to build, with brother Albert, the first airship to be driven by an electric motor.

UNITED KINGDOM

JAMES TYTLER (1745–1804)

The first balloon ascent in Britain was made by the son of a Church of Scotland minister. After attending Edinburgh University James Tytler served as a surgeon on a whaler, and then tried his hand at printing and publishing, before becoming the editor of the 2nd edition of the *Encyclopaedia Britannica*, published in ten volumes between 1777 and 1784. On 27 August 1784 James Tytler flew for half a mile, at about 350ft, over Edinburgh. His last balloon ascent came on 4 October, when large crowds saw him crash.

In December 1792 his publishing activities led him into trouble with the authorities, and he left Scotland, making first for Ireland and then, in 1795, sailing to Massachusetts. He is buried at the East Meeting House, Salem.

VINCENZO LUNARDI (1759–1806)

The second flight in Britain, and the first in England, was made on 15 September 1784 by the twenty-five-year-old Vincenzo Lunardi, who was born at Lucca, in Tuscany. Before a vast crowd, Lunardi rose up from the Honourable Artillery Company's ground at Moorfields; the balloon was a Charlière, made of oiled silk, about 32ft in diameter and equipped with oars and wings. He landed first at Walham Green, took off again, and finally came to rest at Stanton Green End, near Ware, twenty-four miles from the start. Lunardi wrote that during the flight:

When the temperature had fallen from sixty-eight degrees to sixty-one degrees I perceived a great difference in the temperature of the air. I became very cold, and found it necessary to take a few glasses of wine. I likewise ate the leg of chicken, but my bread and other provisions had been rendered useless by being mixed with the sand which I carried as ballast.

Britain promptly succumbed to 'Balloonomania' – there were Lunardi hats, Lunardi garters and many prints showing Lunardi and the balloon; Samuel Wesley composed *A March for the Flight of an Air Balloon*. Lunardi went on to make ascents in Scotland, the north of England, Italy, Spain and Portugal, where he died in July 1806.

In the British Isles, several others had made flights within the next year, including Richard Crosbie who made the first ascent in Ireland at 3.35 p.m. on 19 January 1785. *The Times* reported that the garden at Ranelagh (Dublin) 'was immensely thronged with gentlemen and ladies, and the surrounding fields with tens of thousands of spectators.' Crosbie was dressed in a robe of oiled silk, lined with white fur. His one-piece waistcoat and breeches were quilted in white satin. His outfit was completed by Morocc boots and a leopard-skin hat. The balloon travelled for about four miles before coming down on the beach at Clontarf.

Another early British aeronaut was John Money, an officer of the 9th Regiment of Foot, who made two balloon flights in 1785; his second began at Norwich and ended in the North Sea.

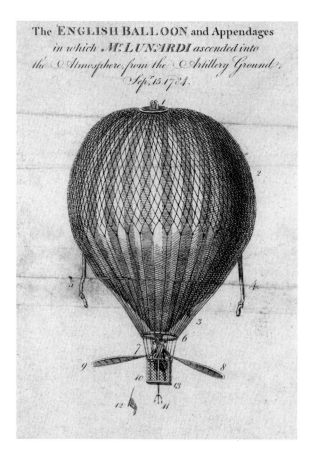

3 The balloon of Vincenzo Lunardi, in which he made the first ascent in England. On 15 September 1784 he took off from the Artillery Ground at Moorfields, London, and finally came to earth near Ware.

JAMES SADLER (1753–1828)

James Sadler became the first English aviator (less than three weeks after Lunardi's flight) on 4 October 1784, in a hot-air balloon which he had made himself. He was in the air for about half an hour, rose to over 3,000ft, and travelled for six miles. For about twenty-five years, from 1785, he did no ballooning, concentrating on building steam engines. He took it up again at the age of fifty-seven, and made nearly fifty ascents in the next five years, often with his son John and then with his son Windham, who was killed in a balloon accident in Lancashire on 29 September 1824.

CHARLES GREEN (1785–1870)

Charles Green, son of a London fruiterer, boosted the development of balloon flight by introducing the use of coal gas. The first ascent in a balloon filled with this gas took place on 19 July 1821 from Green Park in London, when Charles Green exhibited his balloon as part of the celebrations of the coronation of King George IV. Filling a balloon became easier, quicker and cheaper as more streets and houses became lit by gas: the Minutes of the Cardiff Street Commission for 6 November 1828: 'Ordered that the contractor for supplying the town with gas be excused from lighting the town on Thursday the 20th day of November instant, in order that he may supply Mr Green with gas for the inflation of his balloon.' Green also introduced the use of the trail-rope, which was used to control ascending and descending.

By 1835 Charles Green had made over 200 flights. In the following year his *Royal Vauxhall Balloon* was to become famous when, on 9 September 1836, it took nine people up to 13,000ft in nine minutes. Two months later it made a long-distance flight, carrying Green, Thomas Monck Mason and Robert Holland MP (who paid the bills). Aiming for France or Holland, they crossed the Channel in fifty minutes and, after a voyage of eighteen hours, ended up near Weilburg, in the Duchy of Nassau (Germany) – a distance of 580 miles. The balloon was, from then on, exhibited as the *Royal Nassau Balloon*.

In 1840 there was a project to fly across the Atlantic, using a clockwork motor to drive a propeller, but this was abandoned after Green was injured in a landing. He made more altitude trips, and, in November 1852, reached nearly 23,000ft. Charles Green died on 26 March 1870, having made more than 500 balloon ascents. Rolt (1966) described him as 'certainly the greatest English aeronaut and one of the most skilful and successful balloon pilots the world has ever seen.'

GEORGE AND MARGARET GRAHAM

The use of coal gas, and its general availability, led to an increase in the number of balloons, and demonstrations at public events grew more commonplace. George and Margaret Graham were among the growing number of aeronauts touring the country, and found it increasingly difficult to drum up interest now that the novelty had worn off. On 23 June 1825, George Graham made his twenty-fifth ascent (from White Conduit House, Islington), an event unkindly described in the press as 'another of those useless exhibitions, the ascent of a balloon.' The Grahams carried on touring: in November 1825 their balloon came down in the sea off the south Devon coast, and was dragged along for over ten miles before the Royal Marines came to their rescue. M. Cornillot wrote to *The Times* on 19 June 1826, after another Graham exhibition:

The frequency of aerial excursions of late years has naturally worn off the eagerness of curiosity, and abated the excitement which so interesting an exhibition would otherwise not fail to raise; and to this cause we may perhaps attribute the paucity of spectators on the present occasion.

HENRY TRACEY COXWELL AND JAMES GLAISHER

Henry Coxwell was a dentist in Islington. By 1848 he had made fifty balloon ascents, and had become manager of the balloon *Sylph*, touring Britain and Europe with demonstration flights, which included the dropping of bombs.

James Glaisher ran the meteorological service at the Greenwich Royal Observatory, and became the first secretary of the British Meteorological Society.

On 5 September 1862 Coxwell and Glaisher – in a flight financed by the British Association for the Advancement of Science – set a new altitude record of over 30,000ft after taking off from Wolverhampton Gas Works. Glaisher became unconscious and Coxwell lost the use of his hands, but he contrived to pull the valve cord with his teeth so that they were able to drift back to earth near Ludlow.

BRITISH ARMY BALLOONS

Balloons were first built at Woolwich Arsenal in 1878, and balloon detachments accompanied military expeditions to Bechuanaland and Suakin in 1885. By the end of the century the army had a balloon factory and balloon sections stationed at Aldershot. The committee on military ballooning in its *Final Report* (January 1904) recommended that a balloon school should be formed, with eighty-four balloons. It emphasised that, as a matter of urgency, the school should design and build a dirigible balloon – i.e. an airship.

UNITED STATES

JEAN-PIERRE FRANÇOIS BLANCHARD

The first free balloon flight in North America took place on 9 January 1793. It was made at Philadelphia by the Frenchman Jean-Pierre Blanchard, and among the spectators were George Washington and the French ambassador. The envelope was made of varnished silk, with a strong net over it to support the aeronaut's basket. The flight ended in Gloucester County, New Jersey. Four years later Blanchard returned to France.

CHARLES FERSON DURANT

Durant made two tethered ascents in Paris in 1820. A decade later he became the first American to fly in a free balloon, on 9 September 1830, from Castle Garden, New York, to Perth Amboy, New Jersey. He was aloft for two hours, dropping copies of poems on the way. He went on to make eleven more flights.

JOHN WISE (1808–79)

John Wise made his own balloon, in which he first flew on 2 May 1835. He introduced the 'ripping panel': a patch in the top of the balloon's envelope, from which a rip-cord passed down to the gondola. The aeronaut could pull the cord to open the panel, releasing the gas. If this was done just before landing, the balloon deflated, making it less likely that it would be dragged along by the wind.

Wise made plans to cross the Atlantic Ocean in *Atlantic*, his 50,000 cubic feet balloon. The enclosed gondola could accommodate four people, with equipment and provisions, and a lifeboat was carried underneath. A test flight was made on 1/2 July 1859 from St Louis, by Wise, John La Mountain and Oscar A. Gager, who financed the project. Twenty hours later they found themselves coming to earth somewhere east of Lake Ontario, having travelled 1,100 miles (as the crow flies, just over 800 miles), a distance which was not to be surpassed for many years.

John Wise's last ascent was made at the age of seventy-one, with banker George Burn, on 29 September 1879. They were last seen over Lake Michigan. Wise had made over 460 ascents.

THADDEUS C. LOWE

Thaddeus Lowe was another who dreamed of flying across the Atlantic. His balloon was the largest so far: 724,000 cubic feet, 104ft diameter and 200ft from top to bottom. It was first named *City of New York* and then *Great Western* and, like Wise's balloon, carried a lifeboat slung underneath. As it was being filled, the balloon was damaged by a gust of wind, and three weeks later, again while being filled, it exploded. The project was abandoned.

PROFESSOR LOWE MAKING A BALLOON ASCENSION ON A RECONNOITRING EXPEDITION TO VIENNA.—Sketched by our Special Artist.—[See Next Page.]

4 Thaddeus C. Lowe about to ascend in *Intrepid* during the American Civil War. This illustration (from *Harper's Weekly*, 14 December 1861) shows Lowe with General W.E. Smith's division near Vienna, Fairfax County, Virginia.

5 An engraving by E. Morieu, made towards the end of the nineteenth century, showing designs for lighter-than-air machines with some means of propulsion.

In April 1861 Lowe set off on a long-distance flight from Cincinnati. The Civil War had begun and when he landed, after travelling for over 600 miles, the aeronaut was detained on suspicion of being a spy. He was soon released and returned to the north, where Abraham Lincoln put him in charge of military ballooning. By the end of 1861 he was responsible for seven balloons: *Constitution, Eagle, Excelsior, Intrepid, Union, United States* and *Washington*, which had capacities varying from 15,000 to 32,000 cubic feet. As part of his wartime ballooning activities Thaddeus Lowe developed mobile facilities for making hydrogen.

II
THE EARLY DIRIGIBLES

Since the first ascents in 1783 there had been an unsuccessful search for some means of steering, but balloon flight remained subject to the vagaries of the wind, and no balloonist could determine in advance where he or she was going to land. The use of free balloons was limited to sport, entertainment and occasional scientific observations.

From the 1880s there began to appear some reasonably effective steerable balloons, which could be classified into three main types:

A *non-rigid airship* (alternatively known as a *blimp* in later years) has no framework inside the envelope; if it is not filled with gas, the envelope collapses. A gondola is suspended from the envelope.

A *rigid airship* had a metal or wooden framework, over which was stretched the envelope . The lifting gas was contained in *gas cells* or *bags* inside the framework. There could be one or more *gondolas*, or *cars* (carrying crew, equipment and engines) slung under the envelope.

A *semi-rigid airship* has a *keel* fixed along the underneath part of the envelope.

FRANCE

HENRI GIFFARD (1825–82)

Eight years after the first lighter-than-air flight, Erasmus Darwin predicted that 'As the specific levity of air is too great for the support of great burthens by balloons, there seems no probable method of flying conveniently but by steam, or some other explosive material, which another half century may discover.' (*The Botanic Garden: A Poem in Two Parts*, 1791, Part I, Canto I, note to line 254.) The first flight of a powered balloon was indeed accomplished by steam.

Henri Giffard was an engineer engaged in the manufacture of steam engines, who also produced large balloons for tethered ascents by the public. On 24 September 1852, Giffard, wearing a frock-coat and tall hat and cheered on by a large crowd, rose from the Paris Hippodrome in his new balloon. *The Times* (28 September) reported that:

> It is an oblong cylinder, somewhat in the form of a fish, of about 120ft in length, and about 20ft in diameter at its thickest part, and gradually tapering off at both ends. The directing apparatus is a very small and beautifully-finished steam engine, setting in motion a propeller resembling in form the screw used in steam vessels. This is suspended, at about 20ft below the balloon, from a long boom which is attached to it, and which supports at its extremity a triangular sail.

The capacity of the elongated envelope was 88,287 cubic feet; the long pole (or boom) was supported by netting fixed over the envelope. As well as the sail there was a rudder. The gondola supported the pilot and the steam engine, which had been designed by Giffard – it weighed just over 99lb (45kg).

The flight was of about fifteen and a half miles, at an average speed of around 5mph, and the craft went up to 4.900ft. Was it a true dirigible? The weather was good, and Giffard had a certain amount of control over steering, but it could not fly against the wind, and in even a slight breeze it became a free balloon.

ALBERT TISSANDIER (1839–1917) AND GASTON TISSANDIER (1843–99)

In 1881 the Tissandier brothers exhibited a working model of an electric-powered dirigible at the Paris Exposition d'Électricité. They went on to build a full-size version of 37,500 cubic feet – the first airship to be driven by an electric motor. It was just under 92ft long, with a maximum diameter of 30ft, and a new 1.5hp Siemens motor driving a two-bladed pusher propeller. The first flight, of about an hour, was on 8 October 1883 from Auteuil to Saint Germain, at a top speed of 3mph. The next flight was nearly a year later, on 26 September 1884, when the craft was in the air for two hours and travelled for over fifteen miles.

No further work was carried out, perhaps because of the success of Renard and Krebs.

6 The first airship to be driven by an electric motor. Built by the brothers Albert and Gaston Tissandier, it took to the air on 8 October 1883, making the journey from Auteuil to Saint Germain at about 3mph.

7 Albert and Gaston Tissandier standing in the basket of their dirigible.

CHARLES RENARD AND ARTHUR KREBS

Captains Renard and Krebs were engineer officers assigned to the military balloon establishment at Chalais-Meudon. On 9 August 1884 they carried out a successful experiment in 'balloon-steering'. M. Herve Mangon reported on their flight to the Academy of Sciences, declaring that the date 'will remain ever memorable in the annals of discovery'. The non-rigid airship *La France* (66,000 cubic feet) was 165ft long, with a maximum diameter of 27ft. It had an electric motor, producing 10hp to drive a four-bladed propeller. Ascending at Meudon, *La France* flew for about five miles, at a maximum speed of about 20mph, and then returned to its starting point – the first aircraft to do so – and in about twenty-three minutes. This was a great step forward.

La France was to make seven flights in 1884 and 1885.

ALBERTO SANTOS DUMONT (1873–1932)

Alberto Santos Dumont was born in Brazil to a wealthy French father, who moved the family to France when Alberto was eighteen. On 4 July 1898 he made the first ascent in his balloon *Brasil*, which had been built in the workshops of Henri Lachambre at Vaugirard. Alberto's first airship, *Santos Dumont No. 1*, was powered by a 3hp De Dion engine, and was 80ft long x 11ft diameter, with a capacity of 6,400 cubic feet. It took him into the air on 18 September 1898, the first of a series of small non-rigids to be flown by Santos Dumont.

Henri Deutsch de la Meurthe offered a prize for the first person to fly from St Cloud around the Eiffel Tower and back, in half an hour. Santos Dumont made the attempt on 8

8 *La France* at the military aircraft factory at Chalais–Meudon. On 9 August 1884 the airship flew for about twenty minutes and then returned to its starting point – the first aircraft to do so.

9 *Santos Dumont No. 1* made its first flight in Paris on 18 September 1898. It was the first of a series of small airships flown by Alberto Santos Dumont.

August 1901 when his *No.5* airship hit the Trocadéro Hotel, leaving him dangling in the wicker basket, to be rescued by men who clambered over the roofs and pulled him up with ropes. The motor survived in working order.

Santos Dumont No.6 was already being constructed at Vaugirard. Alberto used it to run around Paris; for example, on 13 October 1901 it was parked in front of a café in the Bois de Boulogne until just after 4.00 p.m., when 'le petit Santos' left the café and climbed into the airship's basket. *No.6* ascended, and for five minutes gave a display: it 'mounted, descended, turned right or left, backwards and forwards.' Six days later he won the Deutsch de la Meurthe prize of 100,000 francs by making the flight around the Eiffel Tower.

In February 1902 the airship was to be found in the sea off Monaco. During the flight it had been pitching more than usual and the guide rope, which usually trailed in the water, was yanked up to about 100ft above the surface. Gas leaked from the envelope, the rear part of which caved in, and *No.6* fell into the Mediterranean. The bow end could be seen sticking up above the surface, but the rest of the airship was underwater. (A week later a letter to *The Times* suggested that the pitching might be cured by fitting 'horizontal aeroplanes'.)

Three months later *Santos Dumont No.6* was transported to London in preparation for a display at the Crystal Palace. The envelope was hung from the roof of the Palace and filled with common air. It was then deflated, packed into a basket, and taken to a shed. When it was taken out of its container, gashes were found in the fabric. Scotland Yard was called in, together with army balloon experts, and it was concluded that the silk had perished because it had been dunked in sea-water, inflated with ordinary air, subjected to heat from the glass roof of the Crystal Palace, and then folded up.

Santos Dumont No.7 was damaged in a similar fashion. It was built to take part in the competition for a $100,000 prize at the 1904 Louisiana Purchase Exposition at St Louis. The airship was 164ft long x 26ft diameter. The engine developed 40hp, driving two large propellers, one at each end of the gondola. The envelope was made of two layers of varnished silk. On the night of 27 June the envelope was left in its crate; next morning it was found that the fabric had been slashed. Three days later Santos Dumont left for Paris.

No.9, built in 1903, he named *Balladeuse*. It had a capacity of 7,700 cubic feet, and was described in the *Illustrated Scientific News* of September 1903 by Major Baden-Powell:

> Along each side of the balloon a strip of canvas is sewn, in which is enclosed a number of short battens of wood, and from slings attached to these some 46 steel wires depend to support the frame. The latter, which is 29ft long, is composed of pine rods of triangular section, braced with steel wires and kept apart by wooden triangles of varying size. Toward the front of this frame is the little basket car in which the aeronaut stands, and to the after side of this is fixed the motor.

This was a Clément double-cylinder air-cooled 3hp petrol engine, weighing 26lb.

> The fly wheel is formed of a bicycle wheel, which weighs under two pounds ... The steel shaft runs back from the motor to the propeller at the rear ... The balloon itself weighs only thirty pounds, and the whole apparatus, with framework, car, motor, etc, is under 200 pounds. A tapering tail-rope, 100 feet long, hangs from the front of the balloon and is supported by a pulley under the rear end of the frame, so that balance can be regulated. A large rudder, of 85 square feet, is placed under the after end of the balloon.

Between 1898 and 1906 Santos Dumont had demonstrated, very publicly, that it was possible to produce small airships over which the pilot had a good deal of control. He now turned his attention to another form of flying and on 12 November 1906 his aeroplane, *14-bis*, flew for 722ft in just over twenty-one seconds, the longest powered flight so far achieved by a heavier-than-air machine in Europe.

AUGUSTO SEVERO

Severo was another Brazilian in Paris. His semi-rigid airship *Pax*, built by Lachambre, had a capacity of 70,600 cubic feet, was 99ft long x 15ft diameter, and was driven by a 12hp Bouchet engine. The airship was designed to overcome two of the problems experienced with the Santos Dumont airships: excessive pitching and the collapse of the envelope if the ballonet ceased operating. Severo:

> Balances his balloon by the system of a double screw attached to the balloon itself, two screws which are at either end of an axis that bisects the balloon longitudinally from nose to nose, and which may be worked simultaneously. The rudders are beneath. The position of these screws, attached directly as they are to the balloon, of which they form an integral part, is the essential point distinguishing the Severo balloon from Santos Dumont's. They steady it and prevent it pitching. (*The Times* 9 May 1902)

A rod ran through the envelope from end to end.

On 12 May 1902 Severo and Georges Saché set off from Vaugirard. Both were killed when their craft exploded in flight, falling into the Avenue de Maine. The motor was installed only about 3ft from the envelope, so any escape of gas was likely to be disastrous.

PAUL AND PIERRE LEBAUDY

Lebaudy I: The Lebaudy family had grown wealthy during the nineteenth century through its sugar refining enterprises. In 1902 two members of that family, the brothers Paul and Pierre, decided to finance the construction of a semi-rigid airship designed and built by Henri Julliot and Edouard Surcouf. It was to be of 64,800 cubic feet capacity, 178ft long x 30ft diameter. Major Baden-Powell reported in 1903 that: 'This is probably the most successful aerial machine ever made. It has now accomplished twenty-nine voyages, in all of which, with one exception, it has successfully returned to the point of departure.' The envelope, painted a vivid yellow, was made of two layers of cloth, with a layer of india rubber in between.

> The arrangement, designed by M. Julliot, is quite different to that adopted by so many inventors. There is no long framework suspended below the balloon, but the lower surface of the latter is made flat, and a frame of steel tubing surrounds this plane. From the front part of this six steel tubes run diagonally down the car, set so as to convey the thrust of the propellers to the balloon, the car being supported by a number of steel-wire ropes; below the plane is arranged a keel, consisting of a framework of steel tubing, covered along the after half of it with canvas. This keel is continued far away to the rear, where it ends with the rudder. Under the flat part of the balloon is a layer of uninflammable material, and all the portion above it is occupied by the air-filled ballonet, so there is very little danger of the gas becoming ignited from the engines.

10 *Lebaudy I* at Moisson. It was designed and built for the Lebaudy brothers by Henri Julliot and Edouard Surcouf, and was thought at the time to be 'probably the most successful aerial machine ever made'.

11 *Lebaudy I*. The design did away with the suspended framework of previous dirigibles, substituting a gondola supported by steel wires.

The gondola was made of steel, with the sides partly covered with canvas. A 40hp engine was positioned in the centre, driving two propellers, and achieving a maximum speed of 20mph.

Lebaudy 4/ La Patrie: On 24 November 1907, flown by a crew of five, *La Patrie* left Chalais-Meudon in bad weather for its new base at Verdun, nearly 150 miles away. Their destination was reached in seven hours and five minutes, and the airmen were greeted on arrival by the designer of their airship, Henri Julliot. *La Patrie* was to be lost six days later: at 8.00 in the evening the unmanned airship was being handled by a ground crew of 150 when it broke away.

It was seen eleven hours later, on 1 December 1907, at Llanelli in south Wales, where railwaymen telegraphed to colleagues: 'Watch the airship!' By 8.00 a.m. it had passed over Cardigan and at 1.30 p.m. it hit the ground in Ireland, on James Clokey's farm at Ballysallough, bashing a hole in a dyke, tearing up the ground and losing some bits and pieces. More bits fell off later, including a shaft about 5ft long.

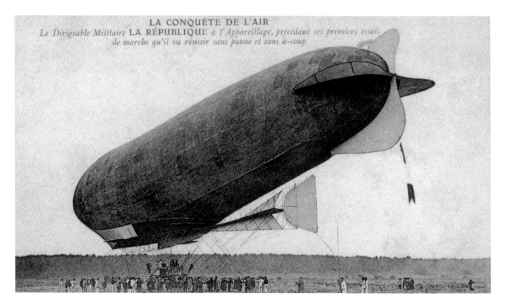

12 The fifth Lebaudy, *La République*, was delivered to the French Army in July 1908, and was based at Chalais-Meudon.

13 Capitaine Marchal, Lieutenant Chauré, Adjudant Vincenot and Adjudant Réau in the gondola of *La République* in September 1909. They were all killed when the airship crashed.

Lebaudy 5/ La République: A similar airship to *La Patrie*, in June 1907 *La République* was put through trials at Moisson, observed by army officers nominated by the Minister of War. It was accepted by the military in July 1908 and sent to the base at Chalais-Meudon. In early September 1909 *La République* left Chalais-Meudon to take part in army exercises, but on the way engine trouble forced a landing, when the airship hit a tree. It was deflated, and continued its journey by rail. After repairs, which took ten days, the craft was able to carry out its reconnaissance role in the exercises. On the flight back to Chalais-Meudon a propeller broke and ripped open a gas cell; there was an explosion and *La République* crashed on to a road, killing the four men on board: Capitaine Marchal, Lieutenant Chauré, Adjudant Réau and Adjudant Vincenot.

Lebaudy 6/Russie: Lebaudy No.6 was 203ft long x 36ft diameter, with a capacity of 128,000 cubic feet, and powered by two 180hp engines. At the end of February 1913 two success-ful trial flights were made, the second of which carried thirteen people, including four Russians. Four months later, after final trials, the airship was accepted by the Russian gov-ernment, taken to pieces, and sent to St Petersburg.

CLÉMENT-BAYARD

The Clément-Bayard Company was founded at Mézières in the Ardennes by Gustave Adolphe Clément, who had been involved in the manufacture of motor cars for many years.

Clément-Bayard I: The company built the engine and gondola of their first airship, and Astra made the envelope (123,500 cubic feet) which had four large 'lobes' at the rear end. A series of successful test flights began in the autumn of 1908, but the French government refused to pay the price asked. Fortunately for Clément-Bayard the Russians were interested, and at 6.30 a.m. on 24 August 1909 the airship left Montesson on its final trial before being handed over to the Russian government. It was caught by a gust of wind, hit a tree on an island and fell into the river at Sartrouville. No one was injured, and by midday the deflated envelope was on board a barge, but the car and engine were still in the river. Everything was salvaged and the airship was rebuilt, going on to be employed by the Russian Army as *Berkut*.

Clément-Bayard II: The second airship, unlike *No.1*, was entirely the work of Clément-Bayard. It was offered to the French government at a far lower price than the first, but again the government would not pay. The *Clément-Bayard II* was sold to Britain in October 1910.

Clément-Bayard III/Adjudant Vincenot: Launched in 1911, this was an airship of 318,000 cubic feet, 287ft long x 44ft diameter, with a maximum speed of about 30mph.

Clément-Bayard IV/Dupuy de Lôme: This military airship, built in 1912, was similar to the *Clément-Bayard III*, but had a capacity of 346,000 cubic feet. Three weeks after the start of the First World War it was shot down by French soldiers.

MALECOT

The *New York Times* of 5 July 1908 published a report from Paris: 'One of the most extraordi-nary flying machines ever seen, even in France, has just completed a successful trial on the army manoeuvre grounds at Issy. This is the Malecot "Aeronef", a peculiar mixture of balloon and aeroplane.' It was 100ft long x 23ft diameter, with a 28hp engine, and carried a crew of three.

ZODIAC

A 'ballooning park' was set up in the Bois de Boulogne in 1897 by the Société Mallet, Melandri and De Pitray. The workshops were soon thriving, and two years later had been renamed *Ateliers de Constructions Maurice Mallet*. In March 1908 Maurice Mallet and Comte de la Vaulx formed the *Societé Française des Ballons Dirigéable*. Their airship *de la Vaulx*, powered by a 16hp Ader engine, was 107ft long x 21ft diameter. Later craft were constructed under the registered name *Zodiac*.

Dirigibles built by Zodiac (dates are of the first flight):

Zodiac No.1/Le Petit Journal
29 November 1908. 24,700 cubic feet. 98ft long x 23ft diameter. With its 16hp Clerget engine it was able to reach 15mph. The envelope of *Le Petit Journal* could be filled with either hydrogen or coal gas.

Zodiac No.2
1909. The gondola was new, but the engine and envelope were from *No.1*.

Zodiac No.3
2 August 1909. In 1910 it was refurbished and sold to the Belgian Army as *Zodiac No.5*.

Zodiac No.4
28 May 1910. Two months later it was at Narrangansett, Rhode Island, the summer home of its purchaser, Stewart Davis.

Zodiac No.6/Duindigt
May 1911. Sold to a private individual in Holland, who presented it to the Dutch army.

Le Temps
March 1911. Bought by subscription and donated to the army as a training ship.

Korshun
17 November 1910. Sold to the Russian Army.

Chaika
8 December 1910. Sold to the Russian Army.

Zodiac XI/ Capitaine Ferber
6 December 1911. Employed by the French Army, it was 250ft long x 42ft diameter, with a capacity of 211,000 cubic feet.

Zodiac Spiess
This was the only French-built rigid airship, and the longest to be constructed before the First World War. It was 370ft long x 44ft diameter; 450,000 cubic feet, with a framework made of wood. The completed craft was not accepted by the army.

Commandant Coutelle
8 May 1913. A military airship of 335,000 cubic feet. 301ft long x 45ft, with two Dansette-Gillet engines, capable of speeds of up to 40mph.

SOCIÉTÉ ASTRA DES CONSTRUCTIONS AERONAUTIQUES

Ville de Paris: This airship was given to the French Army by Henry Deutsch de la Meurthe as a replacement for *La Patrie*, which was lost at the end of November 1907. *Ville de Paris* had a capacity of 114,700 cubic feet, was 196ft long x 34ft diameter, and driven by a 60hp Chenu engine. At the Paris Aeronautical Exhibition of December 1908 visitors saw the dirigible suspended over the central gallery.

Adjudant Réau: The military airship *Adjudant Réau* made a successful flight over Paris on the morning of 10 September 1911. Three months later *Adjudant Réau* reached a height of 7,312ft, a record for dirigibles. Trials continued with a flight carrying eighteen passengers over Paris. By then it had flown well over 600 miles, and had remained airborne for twenty-one hours and twenty minutes. The airship's capacity was 314,000 cubic feet; it was 286ft long x 46ft diameter, and could reach 30mph.

About a dozen Astra airships had been built before the company acquired the rights to the designs of Leonardo Torres Quevado.

Torres Quevado, with army engineer Captain Alfredo Kindelán Duany, had built the first airship for the Spanish Army: *Torres Quevado No.1* first flew in July 1907, and *Torres Quevado No.2* followed in June 1908. Leonardo Torres Quevado moved to Paris, where he rented a hangar at the Astra Company's site at Soutreville. Astra's director, Edouard Surcouf, had been interested in the Spaniard's designs for some time, and a modified *No.2* flew again in October 1909. A contract was signed in February 1910 and production of Astra-Torres airships began in 1911. They could be recognised by their distinctive trefoil-shaped envelope.

On 25 June 1913, just over a year before the outbreak of the First World War, *The Times* published an article in its series *The Powers and Aeronautics*, listing those French military airships in existence, or on order, as well as privately-owned airships which could be requisitioned in wartime. Included were: *Colonel Renard, Ville de Lucerne, Capitaine Ferber, Clément Bayard No.6, Fleurus, Capitaine Marchal, Lieutenant Selle de Beauchamps, Lieutenant Chauré, Adjudant Réau, Commandant Coutelle, Adjudant Vincenot, Dupuy de Lôme* and the rigid *Spiess* (1912).

GERMANY

FRIEDRICH HERMANN WÖLFERT (1852–97)

In 1895 Wölfert fitted an internal combustion engine – an 8hp Daimler – to an airship. The early tests were satisfactory but, five minutes into a flight, on 12 June 1897, his airship caught fire, killing Wölfert and his colleague.

DAVID SCHWARZ (1852–97)

David Schwarz, born in what is now Zagreb, designed the first rigid airship to fly. At the design stage he had offered it to the Austro-Hungarian authorities, but had been turned down. The Russian military attaché became interested, and arranged for Schwarz to continue with his work at St Petersburg in 1890, but it seems that the airship never flew. A second ship was built at Tempelhof, Berlin, but David Schwarz died in 1897, before it was completed.

The airship (about 80ft long x 39ft diameter) had an envelope made of thin sheets of aluminium, which were supplied by the manufacturer Carl Berg   components being made in Berg's factory and assembled at Tempelhof. The envelope was riveted to a framework of lightweight scaffolding, and the gondola was also made of aluminium. The 16hp Daimler engine drove all four propellers: one was on each side of the airship, the main propeller was behind the gondola, and the fourth (used for ascending and descending) was underneath the gondola. Schwarz's widow, Melanie, asked Ernst Jägels to make the first ascent, which took place on 3 November 1897: in a strong wind, the hull leaked gas, and the airship crashed after being airborne for about five minutes. It never flew again, but the Schwarz airship was the first rigid airship and the first with a metal envelope.

HANS GROSS

In June 1906 the Reichstag voted funds for the construction of a semi-rigid airship, designed by Major Hans Gross and engineer Nikolaus Basenach, to be built in the Prussian War Office aircraft works at Tegel, Berlin. An experimental craft took to the air on 29 July 1907, circling around the Reichstag building and then making its way along Unter den Linden. Using the experience gained through building and flying this prototype, another airship was produced (officially numbered *MI*), making its first flight in 1908. It had a capacity of 178,000 cubic feet, and was 233ft long. *MII* was a rebuilt *MI* – in 1909 its length was increased by 10ft and its capacity to 184,000 cubic feet. The airship took part (with a Parseval and a Zeppelin) in army exercises in the Rhine Valley, including a simulated attack on the Ehrenbreitstein fortress at Koblenz. The envelope was badly damaged by fire in September 1913.

MIII appeared in 1909. It was much bigger than the previous two airships: 272ft long, 248,000 cubic feet. In the following year 23ft were added to the length, and the capacity was increased to 320,000 cubic feet.

The 1909 'Kaiser manoeuvres' were to be the largest yet, with 80,000 men, 15,000 horses and 550 guns. They:

> will wage imaginary battles day and night over the plains of Württemberg, Bavaria, and Baden before the War Lord and a galaxy of distinguished foreign guests, including the Archduke Ferdinand of Austria, General Chefket Pasha of Turkey, and Winston S. Churchill of England … The supreme innovation will be supplied by the Gross military airship … It is to have a chance to prove the claim of the Aerial Navigation School that the Zeppelin, Gross and Parseval airships are destined at an early date to supersede cavalry for reconnoitring purposes. (*New York Times*, 12 September 1909)

MIII was destroyed by fire in its shed in October 1912.

CLOUTH

A dirigible was built by the Clouth Rubber Works of Cologne in 1909. It was a small semi-rigid of 65,200 cubic feet, 138ft long x 28ft diameter, able to carry two crew members and four passengers. Rubber was used extensively: for the envelope, the driving belts and the containers for the water ballast. The gondola was made of steel tubing, suspended from the wooden keel. There was one Adler motor-car engine. All the essential controls were duplicated: valves, rudder cables and the belts driving the propellers. The first flight was made to the International Airship Exhibition in Frankfurt, where the dirigible made its way at a low level through the streets. Over the next year the Clouth airship made nearly fifty flights, including a visit to Brussels, covering about 1,200 miles.

AUGUST VON PARSEVAL

Major von Parseval's dirigible made its first ascent at Tegel on 28 May 1906 watched by Karl von Einem, War Minister of Prussia, and his staff officers. The airship circled in the air and then completed several 'figure-of-eight' manoeuvres. Parseval had previously designed the kite observation balloon (with Bartsch von Sigsfeld) which was to be adopted by many armies. Parseval left the army in 1907, so that he could concentrate on the development of flying machines.

In Berlin the Society for the Study of Aeronautics erected a balloon shed in 1907 and the Parseval airship, paid for by the society, made sixteen test flights during that year. A company was formed, the Luftfahrzeugbau Gesellschaft, with works at Bitterfeld, and then a subsidiary to develop passenger airships: Luftverkehrs Gesellschaft.

14 The gondola of the Parseval *PL3* (army designation *PII*). Launched in 1909, the airship was 230ft long x 40ft maximum diameter, with a top speed of 30mph.

Major von Parseval gave a lecture in January 1910 summing up for his Berlin audience the progress to date. The Parsevals launched so far were: a small one of 42,377 cubic feet; *PL1*, owned by the Imperial Aero Club (113,000 cubic feet); *PL2*, a German military airship (given the army number P1), and *PL3*, 'The most important specimen of the Parseval system'. Exhibited at the Frankfurt Airship Exhibition (where it made nearly seventy flights, carrying 600 passengers), it was fast and reliable, powered by two 100hp engines, driving two reversible propellers, each of 13ft diameter. In early October 1909 *PL3* flew Frankfurt–Nürnburg–Augsburg–Munich–Stüttgart–Frankfurt. On this journey it anchored in the open and survived a night of rain and wind without damage. It became army airship *PII*. The smaller *PL4* was built in Austria, bought by the Austrian War Office, and numbered MI.

PL5 was constructed for the Luftverkehrs Gesellschaft, with a length of only 132ft and a capacity of 81,500 cubic feet. In April 1910 the correspondent of *The Times* visited the works at Bitterfeld where he inspected the *PL5*. He reported that the car could hold five or six people, standing close together. 'Vertical steering' was by means of a horizontal rudder near the bow. Control, he wrote, is very simple, 'and although a chauffeur is carried, one man could, at a pinch, attend to the steering, the motor, and the ventilators.' The airship made well over 2,000 passenger-carrying flights, until it was destroyed by fire in June 1911.

PL6 – later known as the *Stollwerck* – appeared in 1909. After reconstruction, its capacity was increased to 320,000 cubic feet.

Susbsequent airships were:

PL7/Griff: 236ft long; 270,000 cubic feet capacity. Accepted by the Russian government after trials at Salisi, near Gatschina, in 1910.

PL8 replaced the destroyed army *PII* (*PL3*).

PL9 and *PL10*: Small craft, built in 1910, and sold to Turkey in 1913. 132ft long, 60,000 cubic feet capacity.

PL11 became army *PIII*. 275ft long; 350,000 cubic feet capacity.

P12/Charlotte was bought by the Rheinisch-Westfälische Flug und Sportsplatz and used for passenger flights and advertising. 260ft long, 302,000 cubic feet capacity.

PL13 was bought by the Japanese government in 1912.

PL14. Completed in 1913 and bought by the Russian government. 280ft long, 355,000 cubic feet capacity. Then there was a run of craft similar to *PL14*. The *PL15* and *PL17* were sold to Italy, *PL16* became army *PIV*; *P18* went to Britain, becoming *Naval Airship No.4*.

OSKAR ERBSLÖH

Oskar Erbslöh became a very experienced balloonist. Born in Elberfeld, at the age of twenty-seven he took part in the 1906 Gordon Bennett Air Race as a representative of the Berlin Aeronautical Society. In 1907 he won the balloon race at St Louis, and in December of that year founded the Rheinisch-Westfälische Motorluft (the Rhenish-Westphalian Aero-engine Company). Erbslöh designed and built the non-rigid airship *Erbslöh*, which was originally 174ft long x 33ft diameter. There were press reports about 'a series of unfortunate accidents' in its first year, and several modifications were made. The airship ascended from Leichlingen on 10 July 1910, only to explode in flight, killing all five on board, including Oskar Erbslöh.

SUCHARD

The German Transatlantic Expedition, financially supported by the chocolate manufacturer Suchard, was a project devised by Joseph Brucker. Born in Austria, but now an American citizen, he was a newspaperman, had been editor of a German language paper in Chicago, and 'Commissioner to Germany' for the St Louis World's Fair.

It was announced that an airship would be built, and by February 1911 it was reported to be 'virtually complete'. After trials it was to be transported to the Cape Verde Islands, ready for an ocean crossing planned to take about three days. The *Suchard* airship was 195ft long x 55ft; 333,480 cubic feet diameter. Because it would be subjected to big temperature changes, the gas would expand and contract a good deal, making it difficult to control the airship's altitude. The trail rope had specially-made buckets attached to it – these could be filled quickly, to try to counteract any rise of the craft. To prevent the gas expansion caused by rises in temperature, sea-water was to be pumped up through a hose, and then sprayed through nozzles to cool down the envelope. The crew of six were housed in the gondola, which was a boat (fitted with two 100hp engines) slung under the envelope.

The airship was named on 15 February by Princess Henry of Prussia and it was planned to start the Atlantic crossing by April. Then it was announced that the Atlantic attempt had been postponed until the autumn, and on 5 May the *New York Times* reported that the *Suchard* was to have started test flights, but these had been prevented by an accident which 'officers and crew think was of malicious origin'. It appeared that valves had been tampered with during the night. Seven months later the paper reported that Joseph Brucker was 'brimming over with confidence' about the voyage, which he said would begin within two months. A correspondent wrote from Berlin that 'The enterprise is regarded with a good deal of scepticism here'.

By November 1911 Dr Paul F. Gans (president and principal financier of the German Transatlantic Expedition) was in New York, informing the press that the purpose of his visit was to see the President and the Secretary of the Navy, in order to finalize arrangements for US Navy vessels to be stationed along the flight path of the *Suchard* airship. He stated that:

> The German Government has a keen eye on the *Suchard*'s movements with a view to determining the usefulness of a dirigible in the event of war. It is my opinion that it would be perfectly possible to mount an airship with guns and bombs and sail long distances into the enemy's country, where it could cause great destruction.

The press was told, in March 1912, that the finishing touches were being put to the airship, and trial flights would be held within a fortnight.

The whole project eventually petered out, and the airship was dismantled.

SIEMENS-SCHUCKERT

The Siemens-Schuckert Werke set up an airship construction department in 1903, and a new airship shed was built at Biesdorf, Berlin, by Karl Janisch. Completed in 1909, it rested on a circular track, so that the whole shed could be revolved to take account of wind direction. It housed the construction of the large non-rigid Siemens-Schuckert airship: 393ft long x 44ft diameter, 476,000 cubic feet. There were three gondolas: the middle one for controlling the airship and for passengers. The front and rear cars each had two 125hp Daimler engines. The front engine in each car turned two propellers, the rear engine one propeller. The first ascent was on 23 January 1911, and the airship went on to make more than seventy flights in about eighteen months. The Siemens-Schuckert was bought by the army, but was soon deleted.

SCHÜTTE-LANZ

The Luftschiffbau Schütte-Lanz was formed at Mannheim on 22 April 1909 by Johann Schütte and Karl Lanz. Schütte was head of the shipbuilding department at the Danzig Technische Hochschule, while Lanz was a manufacturer of wooden products. Their firm went on to construct twenty airships.

The *SL1*, built in the Lanz workshops at Rheinau, near Mannheim, first flew in November 1911. It had a capacity of 688,540 cubic feet, was 429ft long x 54ft maximum diameter, and powered by two 150hp engines. It was a rigid airship, and the first with a framework made of wood. There were three gondolas, the middle one being a cabin for passengers – in a military version this would be replaced by machine-gun platforms. The craft was steered from the front gondola.

The first flight of the year 1912 was at Rheinau, in April: in the forward gondola were Professor Schütte and four engineers; in the rear were six passengers. The airship had ascended to nearly 1,000ft when an engine and the steering failed, causing it to drop to the ground, throwing out the people in the front car – one person was badly hurt. *SL1* rebounded up into the air, carrying the passengers at 5,000ft westward over the Rhine. The other engine stopped, and the airship fell into some trees near Altripp. The envelope and the wooden framework were found to be undamaged, and were brought back over the Rhine by steamer. On 17 July 1913 the *SL1* was wrecked at Schneidemühl, in East Prussia.

SL2 was an army airship, and much bigger: 780,000 cubic feet, 470ft long. There were four gondolas: two fore and aft, plus two side cars.

ZEPPELIN

Ferdinand Adolf August Heinrich, Graf von Zeppelin, was born at Konstanz on 8 July 1838. He decided on an army career and entered the Ludwigsburg military academy at the age of seventeen, travelling to America in 1863 to observe the conduct of the civil war. His first experience of flight, in a tethered balloon, was at St Paul, Minnesota, in August 1863.

Returning to Europe, Count Zeppelin became adjutant to the King of Württemberg and later took part in the Franco-Prussian War. At the age of fifty-two he reluctantly retired from the army. He had become concerned by the development of airships in France, and tried, unsuccessfully, to obtain a subsidy from the state to construct a military airship. Zeppelin enlisted engineer Theodor Kober of the Augsburg Balloon Factory to do the technical work, and in August 1895 they took out a patent for a 'Controllable air-train with several lifting bodies in series'. This was a proposal for an airship in three sections, flexibly joined together.

15 Count Zeppelin.

Three years later a joint-stock company was formed to construct a rigid airship, with Count Zeppelin as the largest shareholder, followed by Carl Berg (the aluminium manufacturer who had been involved with the construction of David Schwarz's airship), Gottlieb Daimler, Max von Eyth, Philip Holzmann, Carl von Linde and Friedrich Voith. Components for the Zeppelin operation were made in Berg's factory and then transported to a floating shed at Manzell, on Lake Constance.

In 1898 work began on *LZ1*: 388,700 cubic feet of hydrogen, contained in seventeen cells. The airship was 420ft long x 38ft diameter, with an aluminium framework, and there were two gondolas, each carrying a 15hp Daimler engine. The airship first flew, with five on board, on 2 July 1900, when it was in the air for seventeen minutes. There were two more flights and then the money ran out. With no likelihood of military orders the undertaking was wound up in February 1901 and all personnel were laid off, with the exception of chief engineer Ludwig Dürr.

Zeppelin made various appeals for money – to magazine readers, to rich people and by organizing a lottery – but with very little success. In spite of this, work began on a new ship – *LZ2* – of 399,000 cubic feet: 420ft long x 38ft diameter. There were problems with the steering gear and the engines, which Daimler had provided free of charge, and in January 1906 they failed again, forcing the airship to come down in a field. There was little damage, but the next night a gale blew up and the *LZ2* was wrecked.

Erster Aufstieg des Luftschiffes Graf Zeppelin am 2. Juli 1900. (Momentaufnahme.)

Das Luftschiff ist 124 m lang. 12 m hoch und ist ca. 200 Ctr. schwer.

16 The first flight of Count Zeppelin's first airship, on 2 July 1900. It was airborne for seventeen minutes.

The first Zeppelin to be bought for military use was *LZ3*. Its dimensions were 446ft x 38ft diameter; 430,780 cubic feet. *LZ3* made a successful two-hour trip on 9 October 1906, with nine people on board, and the army agreed to buy the vessel if it could fly non-stop for twenty-four hours, which it was unable to do. By 1909 *LZ3* had been rebuilt, and was accepted by the army with the official number *Z1*.

LZ4 was subsidized by the government, with the aim of producing an airship which could make a non-stop journey of twenty-four hours. It was larger than the previous Zeppelins, being 446ft long and 532,000 cubic feet. On 1 July 1908 a twelve hour flight was made over southern Germany, and parts of Switzerland and Austria. *The Times* was impressed: 'The voyage of Count Zeppelin's balloon from Friedrichshafen to Basel and Lucerne on 1 July was the greatest achievement of the kind yet attained by a dirigible balloon.'

In early August 1908 *LZ4* began a twenty-four-hour flight to prove itself to the War Ministry. Engine trouble caused a landing at Oppenheim. Ballast was dumped, and the flight went on, against a strong wind. One of the two Daimler engines failed and it was decided to make for Stüttgart and the Daimler works. The airship came down at Echterdingen, near Stüttgart, and Daimler technicians were sent for. While it was being repaired, Count Zeppelin went off to a local hotel, and a crowd gathered to look at the airship. At about 3.00 p.m. a gust of wind lifted one of the gondolas into the air: when it hit the ground an engine exploded, setting fire to the airship. Two or three soldiers were injured, but no one was killed. Count Zeppelin was driven to view the wreckage, and then caught a train back to Friedrichshafen.

The crash resulted in a remarkable phenomenon: within days collections were being organised and money poured in from individuals, industrial firms and banks. So much was raised that Count Zeppelin was able to form a limited liability company, the Luftschiffbau Zeppelin GmbH. Thirty-five-year-old Alfred Colsman was taken on as business manager – he was Karl Berg's son-in-law, and a director of Berg's company which supplied aluminium to Zeppelin. Over 300 acres of land were bought for a new works at Friedrichshafen, and

17 The fourth Zeppelin (*LZ4*) over Lake Constance. On 1 July 1908 it made a twelve-hour flight, described in *The Times* as 'the greatest achievement of the kind yet attained by a dirigible balloon'.

the King of Württemberg gave a further eighty acres, plus a small lake. A large new construction shed was built. The company had by then about ninety employees, with Ludwig Dürr as chief engineer.

Hugo Eckener was put in charge of public relations in 1906, and in 1910 became manager. Born in Flensburg, he had attended the universities of Munich, Berlin and Leipzig, gaining a doctorate in psychology. Eckener was to have a huge influence on the future of the Zeppelin Company.

1909 was a year of development for Zeppelin. In March 1909 the Zeppelin Company set up a subsidiary to make engines, Luftfahrzeug-Motorenbau, with Karl Maybach as technical director. In 1912 the engine works moved from Bissingen am der Enz to Friedrichshafen, and the name was changed to Motorenbau Friedrichshafen – it later changed again to Maybach-Motorenbau.

On 6 October 1909 Prince Henry of Prussia took the chair at a meeting of the board of directors of the Zeppelin Airship Arctic Expedition, which was to be undertaken under the auspices of the German Society for the Exploration of Polar Regions. It was decided that an advance party should be sent, and in the summer of 1910 a group left Kiel for Spitzbergen on the steamer *Mainz* to discover if it might be possible for a Zeppelin airship to fly to the North Pole. On board were Prince Henry, Professors Drygalski and Reich (oceanographers), Professor Miethe of the Technical University of Charlottenburg, Count Zeidlitz (geologist) and Professor Hergesell (an expert on atmospheric currents). In a lecture to a Berlin Scientific Society in February 1911 Professor Drygalski said that 'dirigible ballooning' was not yet sufficiently advanced to make the attempt.

18 The end of *LZ4* on 5 August 1908 at Echterdingen, near Stüttgart.

Phot. Wilcke

19 Dr Hugo Eckener joined the
Zeppelin Company in 1906. Over
many years he was involved in
public relations, fund-raising and
the training of airship crews. He
captained several airships, including
LZ126/Los Angeles and the *Graf
Zeppelin*.

Another development in 1909 was Colsman's suggestion of forming an airline, and in November DELAG (Deutsche Luftschiffahrts Aktien Gesellschaft) was founded. The head office was in Frankfurt-am-Main, with Colsman as business manager, keeping his Zeppelin Company position. Half the capital came from German cities with their mayors on the management board of DELAG. Public relations were in the hands of Dr Eckener, who obtained his airship pilot's licence in February 1911, enabling him to become director of training for DELAG. In the years before the First World War the airline was to operate seven Zeppelin airships: *LZ6*, *LZ7*, *LZ8*, *LZ10*, *LZ11*, *LZ13* and *LZ17*.

LZ6: The first airship to go into service with DELAG was *LZ6*, the last to be built in the floating shed at Manzell. Zeppelin kept trying to interest the military, with publicity flights over Berlin and by enticing Reichstag members to Lake Constance for flights. There was even a visit by Emperor Franz Joseph. But no military orders came, and on 23 August 1910 *LZ6* began the passenger service to Baden-Baden. Three weeks later it burned to destruction in the Baden-Baden shed.

LZ7/Deutschland made two successful flights from Düsseldorf on 25 June 1910, carrying twenty to thirty passengers each time, on the route Düsseldorf–Essen–Dortmund–Bochum–Düsseldorf. Four days later an engine failed and forced a landing into the Teutoburger Forest, near Osnabrück. The airship, which had twenty passengers on board, was wrecked. No passenger was hurt, but one member of the crew was badly injured. Count Zeppelin and his wife made their way to the site, and the remains of *LZ7* were loaded onto trucks and taken to Friedrichshafen.

20 The *LZ7/Deutschland* went into service with DELAG in June 1910. Towards the end of the month, with twenty passengers, it came down in the Teutoburger Forest.

LZ8/ersatz Deutschland: The replacement *Deutschland* – *LZ8* – was being brought out of its shed at Düsseldorf on 16 May 1911, with eight passengers on board, when it was caught by the wind and dashed against the protecting wall in front of the shed entrance. Two cables snapped and the forward part, still inside the shed, lifted up and hit the roof. The airship broke in two, leaving one of the gondolas on the ground outside the shed, while the passengers' cabin hung in mid-air. They were rescued by the fire brigade – no one was hurt.

LZ10/Schwaben: The *Schwaben* made a successful non-stop flight on 6 September 1911, taking seven passengers from Baden-Baden to Gotha, passing over Karlsruhe, Mannheim and Darmstadt.

Schwaben later plied a regular route between Frankfurt and Düsseldorf, where it was destroyed in the early afternoon of 28 June 1912. Caught by a gust of wind, the airship struck the shed, broke in two and exploded.

The subsequent DELAG ships were: *LZ11/Viktoria Luise*, *LZ13/Hansa* and *LZ17/Sachsen*.

The first airship built specifically for the German Navy was *LZ14* (which was given the navy designation *L1*). It was 525ft x 50ft, had a capacity of 776,000 cubic feet, and was driven by three 170hp Maybach engines. *LZ14* first flew on 7 October 1912, and five days later set off on a six-hour flight, travelling 900 miles over north Germany with twenty people on board, including Count Zeppelin.

This Zeppelin went on to make sixty-seven flights before being lost off Heligoland on 11 September 1913 while taking part in fleet exercises. The official account states that the airship was 'thrown downwards by the force of wind from a height of 700 yards'. Ballast and equipment were jettisoned, but the airship hit the water nose first. It then sank, killing six of the crew of twenty.

The *LZ16* (army *ZIV*) was launched as a replacement for army airship *Z1*. On 3 April 1913 the airship left Friedrichshafen to carry out altitude tests before acceptance by the army, with five servicemen and seven civilians on board. It began to experience problems, and in the early afternoon was forced to come down across the French frontier, at Lunéville. This was a sensitive military area, which had been heavily fortified after the Franco-Prussian War. When news of the airship's landing spread an unfriendly crowd gathered, believing that the Germans had been photographing the defences, particularly the fortresses of Manonviller and Épinal. The latter was described as 'a fortress of the greatest possible importance to the defence of France, and its works, all built since 1870, are formidable permanent fortifications' (*Encyclopaedia Britannica*, 1911). Infantry and cavalry were called out to control the crowd gathered round the German airship.

The French government announced that it would look on the incursion as being involuntary, and that the airship must leave France as soon as possible, carrying the civilians only; the officers were to return to Germany by rail. Preparations began – the airship needed repairs, so twenty German workmen were sent from Strasbourg; an engine was taken out to save weight; 200 tubes of hydrogen were delivered. *The Times* reported that on 4 April at 12.30 p.m. 'The German officers, accompanied by the chief of police, left the parade ground in a motor car, escorted through the crowds by a squadron of Dragoons. Stones were thrown.' The airship departed at 12.50 p.m.

This incident provided an opportunity, not to be missed, to take a close look at Germany's latest military airship. *The Times* article went on: 'The airship was minutely examined by General Hirschauer and several other military and aeronautical experts, and also by engineers of Lebaudy and Clément-Bayard, two important French firms, as well as by the expert correspondent of *Le Temps*.' The interior of the vessel was reached by an aluminium ladder from the gondola. 'The frame of the vessel is supported from the inside by a bewildering maze of slender aluminium girders and stays, and in the roof hang gasbags.' An aluminium corridor runs the whole length of the hull; in this are stored 'tools, cables, ropes, and spare parts'. Off the corridor were the captain's cabin, a photographic dark room, a wireless telegraphy cabin, and a lavatory. The two cars below the hull were capable of carrying two machine-guns, and on top of the envelope was a platform, surrounded by netting, intended for a gun. No guns, ammunition or bombing apparatus were found. The details were passed on to the builders of the *Spiess* rigid airship, and to the British.

Three Zeppelins were completed for the navy before the start of the war in August 1914. A scheme for a five-year naval airship program was accepted by the Kaiser in January 1913. Tirpitz's proposal was for two new squadrons, with five airships each; a large base at Nordholz, with four sheds (two of them able to revolve) and subsidies for the construction of civilian sheds, which could be used for military purposes in wartime. The contract for the first airship – *LZ18* – was signed on 30 January 1913. Designated *L2* by the navy, its capacity was 953,000 cubic feet, and it was driven by four 165hp Maybach engines. It first became airborne in September 1913 and was destroyed in October. *LZ18* took off for a test flight from Johannistal, Berlin. On board were fifteen navy men, engineers from the Zeppelin Company, and representatives of the Naval Airship Division – twenty-eight people in all. After ascending for three minutes, flames were seen between the forward engine car and the envelope; in seconds the whole ship was ablaze, and it exploded. As it fell there was another explosion. All aboard died. After the disasters of *L1* and *L2* there were no operational naval airship crews left, although three crews were in training. The scheme to buy ten airships was abandoned, and Peter Strasser (now head of the Naval Airship Division) chartered the DELAG *Sachsen* for training, supervised by Hugo Eckener at the new Fuhlsbüttel (Hamburg) base.

Naval airship *L3* (*LZ24*) made its first flight in May 1913, and *L4* (*LZ27*) in August 1914.

The army also made plans to develop an aviation service. In April 1913 an Army Bill was passed setting out the future organisation of the air forces: Prussia would raise five airship battalions and four aeroplane battalions, to which Saxony was to contribute one airship company and one aeroplane company. Württemburg would also raise an airship company. The locations of the army airship forces would be: *First Airship Battalion* in Berlin, *Second Airship Battalion* – 1st Company: Berlin, 2nd Company in Hannover, 3rd (Saxon) Company in Dresden, *Third Airship Battalion* – 1st Company: Cologne. 2nd Company: Düsseldorf. 3rd Company: Darmstadt. *Fourth Airship Battalion* – 1st Company – in Mannheim. 2nd Company: Metz. 3rd Company: Ulm. 4th (Württemburg) Company: Friedrichshafen. *Fifth Airship Battalion* – 1st Company: Königsberg. 2nd Company: Graudenz. 3rd Company: Schneidemühl.

In addition to these airship stations there were 'private' sheds (which could be requisitioned when necessary) at Baden-Baden, Frankfurt am Main, Gotha, Hamburg, Mannheim, Leipzig and Potsdam.

ITALY

The first Italian airship, that of Count Almerico da Schio (1836–1930), was named *Italia*. It was non-rigid, 124ft long, with a capacity of 42,300 cubic feet. The engine was at first a 12hp Bouchet, later replaced by a 40hp Antoinette which could drive it along at 30mph.

The envelope was made at the Military Aircraft Factory (Stabilimento Construzioni Aeronautico – SCA), run by army engineers at the Cavour Barracks in Rome. The *Italia* first flew, at Schio, in 1905, when it was piloted by Lieutenant Ettore Cianetti.

Gaetano Arturo Crocco and Ottavio Ricaldoni were assigned to develop Italy's first military airship: built at SCA, it made test flights from Vigna di Valle, near Rome, in 1908. It was semi-rigid, 206ft x 32ft, with 97,100 cubic feet capacity. The gondola was boat-shaped, carrying a 100hp Clément-Bayard engine driving two propellers. *No.1* was modified by dividing the envelope into seven gas compartments, with a ballonet in each, and it was lengthened by 23ft or so, to have a capacity of 123,580 cubic feet. *No.1 bis*, as it was called, was taken on its test flight by a crew of five in August 1909.

In the same year another military semi-rigid flew: Enrico Forlanini's *F1/Leonardo da Vinci* (131ft x 46ft; 115,287 cubic feet). The whole keel was enclosed, with a control cabin at the front. The airship could be made to travel astern by reversing the propellers.

In 1909 there also appeared *U1* (semi-rigid, 176ft long, 135,000 cubic feet) constructed by Celestino Usuelli at Bovisa, near Milan. It crashed in 1910, while landing at Verona. Another new dirigible of 1909 was the *Ausonia I* (137ft long, 63,500 cubic feet) of Domenico Piccoli, which was built at Mantua. It was destroyed by a storm in June 1910.

SCA produced the first of a series of 'P' craft between 1909 and 1911: *P1*, *P2* and *P3* were around 200ft long, and of 150,000 cubic feet. In 1909 *P1* made the trip from Bracciano to Naples in three hours, and in 1910 *P2* flew from Rome, across the Appennines, to Venice.

P2 and *P3* were employed in the war with Turkey 1911 to 1912. Tripolitania and Cyrenaica were part of the Ottoman Empire. Italy sent an ultimatum to Turkey on 28 September 1911, stating that Turkey must agree to an Italian military occupation of these territories, or there would be war. The Italians declared war the next day. Early in October Tripoli was shelled from the sea and Tobruk occupied. Turkish forces withdrew into the interior, and the Italians took over Dema, Homs and Benghazi, formally annexing the two provinces on 5 November.

An airship shed was erected at Tripoli in December, but it blew down the next day, damaging the gondola of *P2*. A new airship shed was sent for from Germany, and in March 1912 *P2* made its first flight from Tripoli. By this time there were, in addition to the two airships, twenty-two military aeroplanes with the Italian forces.

In June *La Stampa* of Turin published an account of an airship flight: Commandante Peuco, Captain Saymandi and Lieutenant Benigai set off on what was described as an 'offensive reconnaissance' at 6.00 a.m. They came across an enemy encampment, from which they were fired at with rifles. Two bombs were dropped. The Turks were able to use their artillery against the airship because they had sited their guns on the slopes of sand hills. More bombs were dropped, and the airship returned to base by 8.00 a.m.

By the time the Treaty of Ouchy was signed, ending the war, the airships *P2* and *P3* had made many offensive and observation flights. It was found that, with their ability to stay airborne for up to ten hours, the airships' most useful role had been in reconnaissance and map-making.

P4, *P5 and P6* – Italian Navy airships – first flew in 1912, as did *M1*, a larger semi-rigid craft of 441,370 cubic feet. Powered by two 250hp Fiat engines driving two propellers, it was first flown by the army, before being transferred to the navy. *M1* made a total of 164 flights, before being deleted in 1920. *M2*, also a navy vessel, appeared in 1913.

Test flights of a new Forlanini, to be named *Città di Milano* (236ft x 59ft and with a capacity of 406,000 cubic feet), were made in the summer of 1913. The engines were two 85hp Isotta Fraschini driving two propellers; it was capable of 40mph. Observing the trial flights were two British naval officers, Captain Murray Sueter and Engineering Lieutenant Aldwell. The airship was bought by the city of Milan and presented to the government. It came to grief near Como in April 1914 when, after a mechanical breakdown, it was forced to lose altitude, was blown against trees, and exploded.

By the summer of 1913 the Italian military airships in existence were: *P1, P2, P3, P4, P5, M1* (navy), *M2* (being built for the navy), a *Parseval 17* bought from Germany, and the Forlanini *Città di Milano*.

RUSSIA

Dr Konstantin I. Danielevski, based at Kharkov, experimented with his 'dirigible flying machine' from 1897. It had wings controlled by the aeronaut's muscle power, and a steering arrangement worked by pedals, like a bicycle. Danielevski's machine demonstrated some vertical and horizontal control in calm conditions. In October 1897 he took out a British patent for 'aerial machines with aerostats', suggesting that they could be used for aerial photography, surveying, reconnaissance and bombing.

Eight airships were built in Russia before August 1914, and in addition five were bought from France, and two Parsevals from Germany. *Uchebniy* was a non-rigid (63,500 cubic feet) built at the Russian Army Airship Works, and flown in 1908. The rudder was at the front, and the propeller at the rear. The second army airship came two years later: *Krechet (Falcon)* was 229ft long x 36ft diameter, and with a speed of about 25mph. *Golub (Dove)* of 1910 was constructed at the Igorski engineering works, Kolpino, St Petersburg. It was 150ft long, 78,175 cubic feet capacity, with a speed

21 Dr Konstantin Danielevski with his 'dirigible flying machine' of 1897.

22 Konstantin Danielevski in flight. The wings were worked by muscle-power.

of 30mph. *Yastreb* (*Hawk*) (86,300 cubic feet), designed by A.I. Shabski, was built in Moscow.

In 1912 three new airships took to the air: *Sokol* (165ft long, 86,300 cubic feet) was a product of the Igorski factory in 1911. The De Dion-Bouton engine could drive it along at 35mph. *Kobchik* (158ft long; 60,000 cubic feet) was built at the factory of Duflon, Konstantinovich & Company. *Albatross* came from the Igorski works.

AUSTRIA

The first flight by an Austrian-built airship was made on 26 September 1909 by Alexander and Anatole Renner, in their bright yellow *Estaric*, which was 105ft long, with a 40hp engine. The teenage Renner brothers, who were the sons of an acrobat, had built the dirigible themselves, and *The Times* of London thought that, 'It is characteristically Austrian that the first practical attempt at aerial navigation, as distinguished from mere ballooning, in Austria should be due to the enterprise of two circus lads without scientific training' (*The Times*, 18 October 1909).

The newspaper *Die Zeit* formed a committee, which arranged for a large shed to be erected near the trotting course at the Prater in Vienna. On 17 October around 40,000 spectators gathered on the racecourse, along with the Emperor and members of his family. One observer described the airship as tapering at both ends, and carrying a ladder-like gallery, in the centre of which was the engine. The propeller was at the front, and a large canvas rudder at the back, worked by hand. To ascend or descend the boys changed posi-

tion on the gallery, making the nose of the craft go up or down. The airship n.
about 150ft for over ten minutes.

Next day another ascent was made, in the course of which the dirigible hit the ‿
shed, flinging one of the boys on to its roof. Thus made lighter, the airship rose rap
drifting over Vienna and across the Danube before finally coming to earth at Wagram.

The next outing resulted in an altercation between the army's Airship Detachment
(which had no airship) and the Renner family after the dirigible became tangled up in
some telegraph wires. The cause of this mishap, the Renners said, was the incompetence of
the airship detachment – at this the officer in charge 'marched his men away in a dudgeon'.

The Renner airship made several more successful ascents, and then the family built
another, twice as big, which made demonstration flights around the country.

The first Austrian Army airship was the non-rigid *M1* (Militarluftschiff I), which was the
Parseval *PL4*. Based at the new airship station at Fischamend, near Vienna, it was used for
training until deflated in 1914.

The semi-rigid *MII* was built at Fischamend, to a Lebaudy design.

Another semi-rigid, *MIII*, made its first flight in January 1911. *MIII*'s last ascent was on
20 June 1914, when it took off from Fischamend field. Lieutenant Flatz, in a new Farman
biplane, took off to carry out a simulated attack on the airship. There was a mid-air colli-
sion which killed two in the Farman and seven in the airship.

MIV, designed by Captain Friedrich Boemches, was constructed at Fischamend and was
taken up on test flights in the spring of 1912. The *Austria* (non-rigid, 289,600 cubic feet),
built by Franz Mannsbarth, could carry thirty passengers, and made nearly sixty flights, but
was not taken on charge by the army. It was broken up in 1914.

UNITED KINGDOM

THE SPENCER FAMILY

Edward Spencer (1799–1849), a London solicitor and aeronaut, first went up in a balloon, with
Charles Green, in May 1836 at the Surrey Zoological Gardens. He was to make over a hundred
ascents with Green (including that at Vauxhall Gardens in July 1837 when Robert Cocking was
killed making a parachute jump). Edward's son was named Charles Green Spencer, became
a professional balloonist, and founded 'Charles Green Spencer & Sons: Balloons, Parachutes
and Aerostatic Apparatus of Every description.' Charles Green Spencer's sons – Arthur, Henry,
Herbert, Percival, Sydney and Stanley – all became involved in ballooning.

Percival Spencer first went up in a balloon at the age of eight, with his father, at the
Crystal Palace. He went on to fly over the Channel seven times, and to travel by balloon
from the Isle of Man to Scotland. He gave balloon and parachute demonstrations not
only in Britain but in places such as Egypt, the Straits Settlements, China, Japan and India,
where in 1890 he experimented with a Montgolfier balloon – his 'patent asbestos balloon'
– at Secunderabad. Spencer came down by parachute.

Spencer No.1/Mellin: The first British-built dirigible, the *Spencer No.1* was 93ft long x 24ft
diameter, 30,000 cubic feet capacity, with a 3½hp Simms engine. Underneath was a framework 50ft long. It was known as 'the Mellin airship' because it displayed advertising for this
popular baby food.

At the first attempt, in 1902, the airship failed to rise, but on the evening of 6 July it ascended at the Crystal Palace, where it flew slowly around the polo ground, piloted by Stanley Spencer. The Mellin airship came down, and later took off again carrying Stanley and his nine-year-old niece Maria. These flights were 'witnessed by a large number of Colonial troops and a vast assembly of visitors'.

The next month's attractions at the Crystal Palace included 'Brock's fireworks, the Alaskan Village, the Band of the Coldstream Guards and the Mellin airship'. On 19 September a flight was made over London: Crystal Palace–Chelsea–Earl's Court Exhibition Grounds–Hammersmith–Chiswick–Ealing. After passing over these places, the dirigible came down at Eastcote, near Harrow. *The Times* (22 September 1902) described how a descent was made:

> This, in Mr Spencer's balloon, is accomplished by the gradual displacement of the hydrogen in the balloon by means of a species of enclosed fan, operated by a handle within easy reach of the aeronaut, which pumps, under low pressure, the ordinary air into the envelope, the superfluous hydrogen being discharged at a rent in the side of the balloon.

The dirigible was taken to Blackpool in October, where it waited three weeks for reasonable flying weather before flying, wind-assisted, for about thirty-five miles.

A year later Stanley Spencer was in court: *Spencer Brother's v Mellin's Food Ltd*, before Mr Justice Darling and a jury. Stanley Spencer, trading as Spencer Brothers, sued for £500, which he claimed was owed for advertising Mellin's Food on his airship. The total price agreed had been £1,500. Mellin's had paid £1,000, but refused to pay the rest because, they said, the conditions set out in the agreement had not been met. Mellin's counter-claimed to recover

23 The first airship flight over London. This drawing filled the front page of *The Sphere* of 27 September 1902. The caption read 'Mr Stanley Spencer of the firm of Spencer Bros, aeronauts, at 4.15 on the afternoon of Friday Sept 19, set sail in an airship from the Crystal Palace and journeyed successfully across south and west London to Eastcote, near Harrow.'

the £1,000. Among the conditions of the contract were (a) that the airship should make at least twenty-five return flights, and (b) that, instead of the usual sand or water ballast, leaflets advertising Mellin's Food should be carried, and jettisoned. It was to fly over London 'at an early date'. Ernest Bliss, chairman of Mellin's Food, stated that Spencer should have made flights over the prominent buildings of London, and then returned to his starting point. Spencer lost his case. Mellin's won their counter-claim, and were awarded costs. Five months later a receiving order was made against Stanley Edward Spencer, and he had to attend a bankruptcy examination in April 1904. He was described as an 'aeronaut' whose income came from fees for making ascents in balloons and airships. Spencer stated that he hired the balloons from his brother, and lived in a house belonging to his mother.

Spencer No.2: This was larger than the earlier Spencer airship, but it turned out to be a dud. In December 1904, at Wood Green County Court, engineers of Clayburn & Company sued Auguste Gaudron, of 'Messrs Gaudron & Spencer', for £30, part of the costs of constructing a frame for the airship. Counsel for the defence told the court that 'the ship would not go up, and on two occasions it fell to pieces' at the Crystal Palace. The verdict was in favour of Clayburn. (Spencer's business partner Auguste Eugene Gaudron had been a professional balloonist and balloon-maker in Paris – learning his trade from Lachambre – until joining the Spencer brothers in London in 1890. He was Percival Spencer's son-in-law.)

Spencer No.3: The third Spencer airship was 80ft long x 30ft diameter; 40,000 cubic feet capacity. It had a 5hp Simms motor and a gondola made of wickerwork. Typical flights were made in April and May 1908: Henry and Herbert Spencer took their airship up from the Crystal Palace, watched by big crowd. They ascended to about 1,000ft, circled for five minutes, and then drifted with the wind as far as Keston Mark, near Hayes. In early May the airship was filled with coal gas at Wandsworth Gas Works. The aim was to fly around St Paul's and then go on to the Crystal Palace, but the wind was too strong, so the two aeronauts ended up at Waddon, near Croydon.

The practice of using airships for advertising continued and the latest Spencer airship was hired by Gamage's, the Holborn department store; in December 1908 it carried Mr Talbot (Gamage's aeronautical adviser), Henry Spencer and Herbert Spencer from Wandworth to Holborn – via Battersea, Lambeth and Knightsbridge – where it circled around Gamage's.

Two months later the slogan on one side of the airship read 'Votes for Women', and on the other side 'Women's Freedom League'. This organisation had hired the airship to carry Miss Muriel Matters, one of the leading members of the League. Born in Adelaide, she became involved with the theatre – acting, directing, and teaching elocution. Muriel Matters arrived in London in 1906, joined the Women's Freedom League, and spoke at Speakers' Corner in Hyde Park, and in 1908 travelled around the countryside with the 'Votes for Women' caravan. In October of that year, as part of a protest in the chamber of the House of Commons, she chained herself to a grill in the gallery. Miss Matters, still attached to the grill, was eventually removed. She was to spend a month in Holloway gaol, having been arrested for 'disorderly conduct'.

16 February 1909 was the day of the state opening of Parliament by the king, Edward VII. The plan was for the 'Votes for Women' airship to appear over the Houses of Parliament, when leaflets would be dropped and the crowds addressed through a megaphone. The plan could not be carried out because of the wind – the airship did not appear over the royal procession, but was carried off on a two-hour flight over Wormwood Scrubs, South Kensington, Tooting and Coulsdon. Supporters followed in a motor car, following the trail of leaflets dropped by Muriel Matters.

MISS MUREIL MATTERS,
With the Megaphone Through Which She Was to Have
Addressed the Lords and Commons.

24 Muriel Matters in the basket of *Spencer No.3* on 16 February 1909. The airship carried the slogan 'Votes for Women' and the intention was to drop leaflets to the crowds gathered for the state opening of Parliament.

One year on, and the airship was advertising *Carbic* – a new acetyline generator. An ascent was made from Wandsworth gasworks with the aim of flying over the Aeronautical Show at Olympia, and then on to St Paul's, where crowds had gathered to see the airship. On board were Henry Spencer and two passengers. The engine worked for five minutes, then stopped. The *Carbic* airship was now a free balloon, and was blown over Chelsea and Hyde Park. It just cleared the housetops at Marble Arch, continued on its way and ended up in Essex, near Nazeing Common. The propeller was broken when the airship hit a fence on landing, but no one was hurt.

In the summer of 1913 Herbert and Stanley Spencer made a number of sorties over London, with the exhortation: 'Give him Bovril!'

FRANCIS ALEXANDER BARTON

The sub-title of Barton's autobiography describes him as a 'medical doctor, airship and hydroplane engineer, inventor, market gardener and traveller'. The son of a doctor, he attended Harrow School, Cambridge University and St George's Hospital, before setting up as a medical practitioner at Beckenham. In 1902, with Auguste Gaudron, Barton went up in a balloon to celebrate the coronation of Edward VII, occasionally throwing out stamped postcards. The aeronauts were blown from Beckenham over the Channel, splashing down just off the French coast.

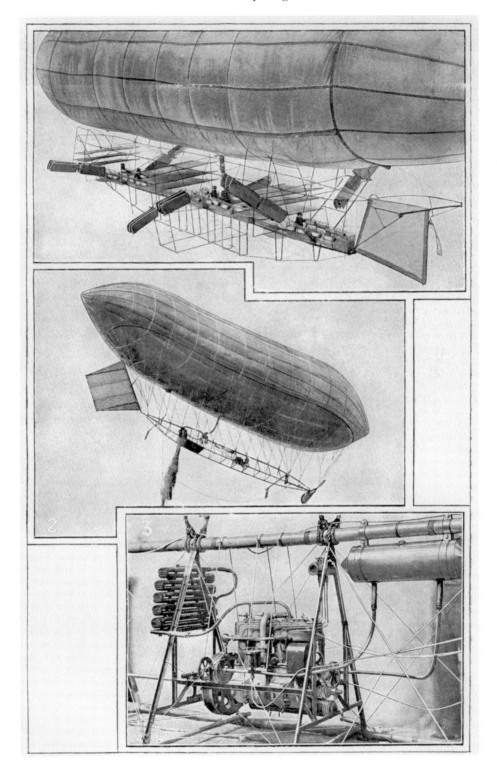

25 *Top*: The airship of Dr F.A. Barton, 1905. *Centre*: 'Mr Spencer restoring the equilibrium of his airship' by jettisoning ballast. *Bottom*: The Simms engine installed in the Spencer airship.

Dr Barton was interested in developing a dirigible and, from 1899, had made trial flights with models in Beckenham Public Hall and then in the open air, before enlisting the aid of Spencer Brothers. Construction began at Alexandra Palace in 1903. Barton's semi-rigid airship was 170ft long x 40ft diameter; 170,000 cubic feet capacity. The envelope was made of varnished silk, and was divided internally into three compartments by the use of flexible partitions. The envelope also contained a ballonet, which could hold 12,000 cubic feet of air. Underneath the envelope was a framework (140ft long, made of bamboo, with wire stays) which supported a walkway and three 50hp Bouchet engines. Sets of moveable 'aeroplanes' were fitted as an aid to stability, and to assist in ascending and descending. The rudder measured 17ft x 12ft. One writer described the airship as 'very big and cumbersome', but the War Office had stated, in 1901, that it would be bought for the army if certain conditions were met – one being that the craft could turn in a circle of 100 yards radius.

A tethered ascent was made on 12 July 1905, to 'test the engines and aeroplanes'. Present were Dr Barton, consulting engineer F.L. Rawson, and Messrs. Gaudron and Spencer. Eleven days later came the first, and only, public ascent, in the grounds of Alexandra Palace. Various modifications had been made: the airship was now 180ft long and had a capacity of 190,000 cubic feet. Underneath the envelope the framework had been shortened by 13ft. There were two Bouchet engines, connected by belts to four propellers which were smaller than the originals, on the advice of F.L. Rawson. The display disappointed the large crowd – the airship simply drifted away sideways in the wind. The next annual general meeting of the trustees of Alexandra Park heard that 'the Barton airship resulted in a loss to the trustees of £327'.

ERNEST THOMPSON WILLOWS

Ernest Willows, born in 1886, was the son of Joseph Thompson Willows, a Cardiff dentist. Ernest began training to follow the same occupation as his father, but grew more interested in aeronautics, designing his first dirigible when he was nineteen: *Willows 1* (74ft long x 18ft diameter; 12,000 cubic feet capacity) took to the air in the summer of 1905, powered by a 7hp Peugeot engine. The *Willows 2* was 80ft long x 22ft diameter, 20,000 cubic feet. It had a 39hp JAP engine driving two wooden Handley Page propellers. On 4 June 1910, Willows flew from his shed at Cardiff's East Moors to the city centre at Cathays Park, where the airship stayed for about half an hour. He was at Cheltenham in July, making exhibition flights and when these had finished he flew home to Cardiff in four hours, passing over Chepstow and Newport.

On Saturday 6 August he took *Willows 2* on a much longer flight: the 150 miles from Cardiff to London, in ten hours. He had intended to start two days earlier, but the envelope was damaged in its shed – stones had been thrown at it. With repairs completed, Ernest Willows set off at 8.00 p.m. on Saturday evening. After crossing the Bristol Channel, he looked out for 'an illuminated motor car' in which his father and two mechanics hoped to guide him to the capital, but Ernest soon lost sight of them.

Flying along at about 15mph he passed Bath, Marlborough and Hungerford, rising to 2,600ft over Reading. At Esher he dropped down and spoke to a railwayman, who suggested that Willows should follow the London & South-Western Railway line. He intended to land at the Crystal Palace, and came within 200 yards, but by then he had run out of fuel and the engine had stopped. Ernest Willows threw out a grapple, which caught in a tree, but the rope snapped. *Willows 2* was blown for about five miles over Catford and Hither Green as far as Mottingham. The envelope was found to be leaking, because of the

26 *Willows 2* in front of City Hall, Cardiff, on 4 June 1910.

27 Ernest Willows in *Willows 2*.

vandalism at Cardiff, so time had to be spent on repairs. While this was going on thousands of people turned up and, for sixpence a head, were able to have a close look. A half-hour trip took the airship to the Crystal Palace.

The headlines in the *New York Times* of 8 August read 'Night Flight to London' and 'Welshman in Dirigible Sails from Cardiff to London, 150 miles'. A special cable reported: 'A voyage from Cardiff to London in a dirigible balloon was made last night by Ernest Thompson Willows, a slight, boyish-looking native of Cardiff. This is the longest flight by a dirigible at night and longest of any kind ever made by such a machine in England.'

Willows 3/City of Cardiff: Soon after this flight Ernest Willows met Russell Besley, manager of the North British Rubber Company, and told him that he wanted to build a larger airship, capable of taking him to Paris. The manager showed his firm's catalogue to Willows, and recommended that their No. 3 fabric would be suitable for the envelope. This was selected. In September 1910 a committee was formed to assist the new project: chairman was D. A. Thomas (later Lord Rhondda, owner of the Cambrian Collieries), Treasurer Lord Ninian Crichton-Stuart (who was to die five years later at the battle of Loos). Their aim was to raise at least £6,000.

The Willows airship was housed, together with the *Clément-Bayard II*, in the *Daily Mail* shed at Wormwood Scrubs. By October it had been provided with a 35hp JAP engine, and a new envelope of rubber and cotton (capacity 32,000 cubic metres) made in a gallery of the Crystal Palace.

The first flight of *Willows 3* was made on 29 October 1910, and on 4 November E. T. Willows and Frank Goodden made the first dirigible flight from England to France. They ascended from Wormwood Scrubs at 3.25 p.m., hoping to reach Paris, but were forced to land near Douai at 2.00 a.m. next day. The wind was too strong for the airship, so it was deflated, packed up and taken to a garage. Customs officers turned up and demanded that Willows pay import duty on the gas in his airship, but the director of customs relented after representations from the French Aero Club, provided that the airship did not stay permanently in France. Willows later took his airship to Paris, where it made flights around the Eiffel Tower and over the city. Ernest Willows stayed in France until early January, when he returned to England, taking the envelope with him.

In March 1911 Willows was contracted to give exhibition flights at Wolverhampton, but the envelope was leaking and he could not fulfil his contract. In May 1913 he began a flight from Wolverhampton to London, but the envelope was still leaking so the airship had to come down at Leamington. A year later Willows was sued by the North British Rubber Company for £253 still outstanding for the envelope material (they had already been paid £244). Willows counter-claimed for damages of £600 because the envelope became useless through leakage. In court the company's representative said that the envelope should not have been covered with linseed oil varnish, as this destroyed rubber; furthermore, the cover had been damaged by poor packing and damp. Mr Justice Scruton gave judgement, with costs, for the North British Rubber Company.

A meeting of the creditors of Ernest Willows, 'aeronautical engineer', was held in Birmingham: his liabilities were £1,409; his assets were just over £10. It was stated that his financial failure was due to the costs of the law case. Ernest Willows did not attend, but sent a telegram to say that he had missed his train.

Willows 4: 20,000 cubic feet capacity; 90ft long x 20ft diameter. *Willows 4* first flew in 1912, and became *Naval Airship No. 2*, with a larger capacity of 39,000 cubic feet. It was used for training purposes.

Le Petit Journal

ADMINISTRATION
61, RUE LAFAYETTE, 61

Les manuscrits ne sont pas rendus

On s'abonne sans frais
dans tous les bureaux de poste

5 CENT. SUPPLÉMENT ILLUSTRÉ 5 CENT.

21ᵐᵉ Année — Numéro 1.044

DIMANCHE 20 NOVEMBRE 1910

ABONNEMENTS

SIX MOIS · UN AN
SEINE et SEINE-ET-OISE.. 2 fr. 3 fr. 50
DÉPARTEMENTS.......... 2 fr. 4 fr. »
ÉTRANGER .... 2 50 5 fr. »

COMMENT SONT ACCUEILLIS EN FRANCE LES CONQUÉRANTS DE L'AIR

A peine l'aéronaute anglais Willows a-t-il atterri, qu'il reçoit la visite d'un agent du fisc

28 The front page of *Le Petit Journal* of 20 November 1910. Having just flown from London to France in *Willows 3*, Ernest Willows is confronted by a customs official with a demand for payment of import duty on the gas in his airship.

Willows No.5: Launched in 1913, with a capacity of 70,000 cubic feet, *No.5* was 140ft long x 30ft diameter, and powered by a 90hp Curtiss engine. It made very few flights.

BRITISH MILITARY AIRSHIPS

In the first year of the twentieth century the superintendent of the Balloon Factory, Colonel J.L.B. Templer, visited Santos Dumont and the Lachambre balloon factory in Paris. He also met Captain Renard of the Chalais-Meudon military ballooning establishment. Templer's report on his visit pointed out that Santos Dumont had demonstrated the practicability of the dirigible balloon and recommended that Britain should become involved with this new technology. Three years later, in January 1904, the *Final Report of the Committee on Military Ballooning* (Secretary: Lieutenant-Colonel J.E. Capper) recommended that the Balloon Factory should produce a 'dirigible balloon' as a matter of urgency. The Balloon Factory was moved from Aldershot to Farnborough, where an airship shed was erected; the balloon shed was brought from Aldershot and put up next to the new shed. Later in 1904 Colonel Capper spent a month at the St Louis World's Fair investigating aviation developments and talking to pioneers such as the Wright brothers and Octave Chanute. Colonel Templer retired from the Balloon Factory in May 1906, but stayed on as an 'adviser'. He was replaced by Colonel Capper, who became 'Officer Commanding, Balloon School and Balloon Factory'.

Nulli Secundus (Dirigible No.1): This was the army's first airship *Nulli Secundus* 'Second to None' was 122ft long x 25ft diameter, with a 50,000-55,000 cubic feet capacity. It was designed by Templer, with S.F. Cody responsible for the propellers, shaft, and engine – an Antoinette which Cody bought in France. The envelope, which had been made at the Balloon Factory, consisted of a dozen layers of goldbeaters' skin. (Goldbeaters' skin was made from the outer membrane of the large intestine of cattle.)

Four 'saddlebands' (each 4ft wide) went round the envelope to support the framework, made of steel tubing, slung below. This framework was also supported by a net, which covered the envelope.

The *Automotor Journal* described its first appearance, on 10 September 1907: 'At 10.00 a.m. the great doors slid open and the huge caged monster was brought blinking into the sunlight.' On a short test flight, the dirigible was manned by Capper, Cody and Captain King (Chief Instructor, Ballooning). It was airborne again in the afternoon.

Three weeks later, after the addition of a tailplane, *Nulli Secundus* was in the air for fifty minutes, covering twelve miles.

By early October it had been decided to undertake a publicity flight over London (where the airship would be seen by thousands) even though it had been in the air for a total of only three hours, and there were continuing problems with the engine. It was realised that a contrary wind might make the return leg difficult, if not impossible. Nevertheless, Capper and Cody took off at 10.40 a.m., with a ground crew following in Cody's motor car. The route flown was: Frimley–Bagshot–Sunningdale–Staines–Hounslow–Brentford–Kensington Palace–Hyde Park–Buckingham Palace–the War Office(*Nulli Secundus* flew along Whitehall at 850ft, watched by members of the Army Council)–Trafalgar Square–Strand–Fleet Street–around St Paul's (at 12.20 p.m.)–Kennington Oval–Clapham Common (1.10 p.m.). Here they came up against a headwind, and manoeuvred and hovered over the common for about half an hour. They could not land because of the crowds, so they set off for Sydenham, landing at the Crystal Palace at 2.07 p.m. The army's new airship had been in the air for three hours and fifty minutes, flying fifty miles.

1024. - Le Ballon Dirigeable Anglais " Nulli Secundus " - Vue arrière J. H.

29 The British Army's first airship, *Dirigible No. 1*, otherwise known as *Nulli Secundus* (Second to None). Over 120ft long, it first flew on 10 September 1907.

The airship was made secure in the middle of the cycle track and was left in the care of soldiers of the Royal Engineers, commanded by Sergeant Ramsay. Colonel Capper held a press conference, at which he said that 'it was better to be travelling in an airship than motoring on the roads, there being no speed limit and no dust.' He summed up:

> We do not pretend that this is a first-class man-of-war of the air, but we have at least learned how an airship is to be managed, and we know more or less what is wanted. For a first attempt and with a gas bag made five years ago by Colonel Templer I think it is quite satisfactory in comparison with what foreign nations have done in this direction.

Hydrogen had to be brought from Farnborough and the weather was, in any case, too bad for flying, so *Nulli Secundus* stayed on the ground. On 10 October it looked as if the airship would break loose in the strong wind, and there was:

> …severe damage to the framework between the car and the balloon, the steel rods of which it was composed being bent and broken into many pieces … All the workpeople in the grounds at the time were summoned, and policemen, gatemen and other workers assisted the airship's guard in holding the vessel down. It was then found imperative, to avoid further damage, that *Nulli Secundus* should be deflated. The valves were opened by Sargeant Ramsay, and the hydrogen gas was allowed gradually to escape. (*The Times*, 11 October 1907)

The engine was taken out 'and laid undamaged upon the grass, and the envelope of the balloon lay coiled up nearby. By 11 o'clock the airship was reduced to a framework. The envelope, engine, and the parts of the framework were removed by a motor-trolley, which had been telegraphed for from Aldershot.'

Nulli Secundus II: The airship was rebuilt, with the same envelope and engine, but the net covering the envelope was replaced by silk sheeting, which it was hoped would give more protection to the goldbeaters' skin. The saddle bands, which were fixed over the silk, were made narrower. Some flights were made in July and August 1908, but there were still problems with the engine. The envelope was deflated, and the engine was installed in Cody's aeroplane, for which it had originally been intended. In October 1908 *British Army Aeroplane No. 1*, designed by S.F Cody, made the first powered aeroplane flight in Britain.

The Advisory Committee for Aeronautics, set up by the government in 1909, recommended that the navy should be responsible for any rigid airships, and the army should continue with smaller dirigibles and aeroplanes. The Balloon Factory and the School of Ballooning were separated: Lieutenant Colonel Mervyn O'Gorman became superintendent of the Balloon Factory (which was manned by civilians); the School of Ballooning was to be commanded by Colonel Capper, later replaced by Major Sir Alexander Bannerman.

On 1 April 1911 the School of Ballooning was expanded into the Air Battalion Royal Engineers (commanded by Bannerman), which had fifteen officers and 150 men. No. 1 Company (Airships) – Captain Edward Maitland – was at Farnborough; No. 2 Company (Aeroplanes) – Captain John Fulton – was stationed at Larkhill, on Salisbury Plain.

Baby: Designed and built under the supervision of Colonel Capper, work began in 1908. Nine layers of goldbeaters' skin made an envelope of 21,000 cubic feet capacity; a ballonet was installed, which could hold 3,000 cubic feet of air, pumped in by a fan. *Baby* was 81ft long x 24ft diameter. Originally two Berliet engines were fitted, driving a two-bladed propeller. From May 1909 until the end of the year about a dozen flights were made.

Beta: Baby was developed, and renamed *Beta* (the first of four army non-rigids to be identified by letters of the Greek alphabet). Its capacity was now 35,000 cubic feet, and with a 35hp engine it could achieve 20 to 30mph. Early in June 1910 it flew from Farnborough to Southwark Bridge in London, and back again, in about four and a quarter hours, round-

30 *Beta* was the first of the British Army airships to be identified by a letter of the Greek alphabet. Early in June 1910 it flew from Farnborough to Southwark and back in about four and a half hours.

ing St Paul's on the way. On board were Colonel Capper, Lieutenant C.M. Waterlow (Balloon Company, Royal Engineers) and Theodore John Ridge (Assistant superintendent of the Balloon Factory, who was also a lieutenant in the London Balloon Company, Territorial Royal Engineers). Five weeks later a similar trip was made; this time *Beta* carried Lieutenant Brooke Smith, Lieutenant Ridge and Sergeant Ramsay. Next day it broke down near Andover, landing in a field near Abbots Ann. Spare parts and gas were sent for, and a number of mechanics and other soldiers arrived. *Beta* was then moved to a local foundry about two miles away and repaired overnight.

Beta carried a Marconi spark wireless apparatus, and messages were sent between airship and its headquarters for the first time in January 1911, over a distance of twenty miles from Alton to the Balloon Factory at Farnborough. On the same flight S.F. Cody acted as escort, flying his aeroplane nearly twice as fast as the airship.

Beta was given a variety of tasks during 1913, including artillery observation, a parachute jump by Captain Maitland, and giving a half-hour flight to the Prince of Wales.

Gamma: The envelope was made in Paris, of rubberised fabric made by a Hannover company. The colour was bright yellow, and the airship became known therefore as *The Yellow Peril*. It was 152ft long x 30ft diameter, 75,000 cubic feet capacity, and with its 80hp Green engine *Gamma* had a top speed of nearly 30mph. The first flight was made on 12 February 1910. During 1912 the airship could have been seen at Chatham and Wormwood Scrubs, and in the September participated in army exercises on Salisbury Plain, after which *Gamma* went on to 'bomb' Cambridge.

Gamma was passed to the Royal Navy in 1913, and scrapped on 16 May of that year.

Clément-Bayard II: This French airship would be bought by the British War Office if it could meet the specifications drawn up by a group of experts, which included Colonel John Capper, Mervyn O'Gorman and the chairman of the Advisory Committee for Aeronautics. Among the stipulations were that the dirigible must: (1) carry six crew members and nec-

31 Army airship *Gamma* made its first flight in February 1910. It was transferred to the navy in 1913 and scrapped in May of that year.

CAR OF BRITISH AIRSHIP GAMMA   3401·3

17 Airship Gamma.   May & Co. Aldershot. 2.

32 The gondola of the army airship *Gamma*.

essary equipment, (2) have two engines of equal horsepower, (3) have a ballonet capacity of twenty-five per cent of the total capacity, (4) be easy to deflate, dismantle and load on to wagons, (5) be capable of being walked out of its shed by a maximum of thirty men, (6) be robust enough to be anchored in the open in winds of up to 20mph for twenty-four hours, (7) be able to fly up to 6,000ft, fully manned, and with wireless apparatus installed, (8) complete a triangular course of 100 miles each side in under fourteen hours, of which four hours must be at more than 3,000ft, (9) achieve 32mph over five miles.

Monsieur Clément wanted £25,000 for his airship, but the War Officerefused to pay this. A price was agreed of £22,000, provided that a new and larger envelope was fitted. The sale was, of course, subject to the achievement of the original criteria, but Clément-Bayard 'demurred as to the conditions of the tests'. The War Office then offered £18,000 for the craft with the old envelope, provided it could pass the tests. Clément refused.

The War Office then offered to waive the tests, and would buy the airship as it stood for £12,000, plus the cost of bringing it to London. Clément refused. The Parliamentary Aerial Defence Committee offered to pay the balance between the British offer and the French demand (Arthur du Cros MP, who had been a strong advocate of the purchase, contributed a large sum). Clément accepted.

The French dirigible flew to Wormwood Scrubs on 15 October 1910 – the first airship to cross from France to Britain. It was to be accommodated in the *Daily Mail* shed, which was 354ft long x 76ft wide x 98ft high. Two galleries, reached by ladder, ran around the interior. One end of the shed was open, but it could be closed off by a large canvas curtain.

The *Clément-Bayard II* was formally handed over to the War Office on 29 October. It was found that the envelope leaked badly, and the airship was dismantled, never to fly again.

Lebaudy 9/Morning Post: This semi-rigid airship was bought by the readers of the *Morning Post* as a gift to the British Army, subject to the same criteria laid down for the Clément-Bayard. Built at Moisson by Lebaudy Brothers, with Henri Julliot as chief engineer, the capacity was 353,166 cubic feet, and it was fitted with three ballonets. Two 16ft-diameter propellers were driven by two 135hp Panhard petrol engines. The airship was 337ft long x 39ft diameter. The gondola was made of steel tubes, and could carry twenty people. It was supplied with a 'landing pivot' – a steel tube at the bow; when the airship was moored this pivot was the only part in contact with the ground, making it easier to swing the craft round.

The five-and-a-quarter-hour journey from France to Farnborough began at 10.15 a.m. on 26 October 1910. On board were Major Sir Alexander Bannerman (commanding officer of the School of Ballooning), the pilots Louis Capazza and Henri Julliot, Mr Allen (Paris correspondent of the *Morning Post*) and three engineers. As a precaution, a destroyer was stationed in the Channel.

This was the largest airship yet seen in Britain, and there was great excitement in Brighton as the Lebaudy passed over the Palace Pier and the town centre. At 3.07 p.m. the airship was spotted by a Farnborough look-out man perched on top of the large airship shed, above a big crowd which included many senior army officers.

The landing place was marked on the ground by a large white cross, made of linen. Three ropes were let down from the airship, and grabbed by a dozen Coldstream guardsmen – the craft rose unexpectedly and one man was lifted into the air, but he fell into a bush without coming to any harm. With Bannerman shouting instructions from the gondola, the airship was then hauled down.

When the airship was walked into the shed (which had been completed earlier in the year) it was found that the roof was, unfortunately, 10ft too low, and the Lebaudy's envelope was ripped on a girder. The airship finally came to grief in May 1911 when it collapsed on trees near a house at Aldershot. Seven were on board, but no one was injured. It had not yet been taken on charge by the army, so the government refused to pay the £4,000 repair bill.

Delta: Delta (175,000 cubic capacity. 198ft long x 39ft diameter) was launched at Farnborough in September 1912, with two Coventry-made White and Poppe engines. Acceptance trials were not completed for over a year until, on 10 October 1913, *Delta* left Farnborough at 6.30 a.m. under the command of Captain Waterlow. The flight took the airship over Redhill, Sheerness, Chatham, London (round St Paul's), and back to Farnborough at 3.30 p.m. *Delta* was then taken over by the Military Wing of the Royal Flying Corps, later becoming *Naval Airship No.19.*

The government's *Memorandum on Naval and Military Aviation* (Cd 6067) was published on 12 April 1912. It led to the formation of the Royal Flying Corps, composed of a Naval Wing and a Military Wing of seven aeroplane squadrons (with twelve aeroplanes each), plus one *Airship and Kite Squadron* (providing two airships and two flights of man-bearing observation kites). The *Memorandum* stated that 'The airship possesses a great advantage over the aeroplane in military warfare of being able to receive messages by wireless telegraphy; it is able to transmit to greater distances.'

By this time the Royal Aero Club had issued licences to eight dirigible pilots of whom only one – Ernest Willows – was a civilian. To train more pilots a Central Flying School was opened on 17 August 1912, and its first pilots graduated a week later. An Admiralty Air Department (director: Captain Murray Sueter) was formed in November 1912.

At the end of 1913 the RFC's Military Wing airships were transferred to the RFC's Naval Wing.

The Army Aircraft Factory at Farnborough was renamed The Royal Aircraft Factory. At this time a visitor would have seen a large group of buildings which included drawing offices, test facilities, a chemistry laboratory and a balloon and airship factory, with a hydrogen-making plant, an aeroplane workshop, engine test-beds, and hangars for aeroplanes and airships. It had recently designed a portable airship shed, made of iron and canvas, which could be erected in a fortnight to house a dirigible of up to 160,000 cubic feet.

Eta: Launched by the Royal Aircraft Factory in August 1912, it was 188ft long x 33ft diameter; 118,000 cubic feet. It was powered by two 80hp Canton-Unné engines. The Royal Aircraft Factory had developed what became known as *Eta patches*, which meant that the gondola could be suspended directly from the envelope, and not from some kind of net. This airship was employed on cross-country flights (on one of these *Eta* towed the Willows *Naval Airship No.2* – its engine had stopped – back to Farnborough), army exercises and experiments in wireless communication. It was later used for training, as *Naval Airship No.20*.

His Majesty's Airship No.1: HMA *No.1* was built as an experimental dirigible – the first British rigid airship. The specification stated that it must be capable of undertaking twenty-four-hour patrols, and achieve 40knots. The new airship was to be 512ft long x 48ft diameter, with a capacity of 663,000 cubic feet. Work began in 1909, with Vickers in charge of constructing the duralumin framework. Vickers had been selected because of their experience with building submarines – the navy's first submarine had been launched at Barrow-in-Furness eight years earlier.

The Admiralty was responsible for fitting the rudders and planes, and for the seventeen gasbags and the envelope, which was made of waterproofed silk. The upper part of the envelope was silver, and the lower half yellow. The two 80hp engines were made in Birmingham by the Wolseley Tool and Motor Car Company, a subsidiary of Vickers. *HMA No.1* became popularly known as *Mayfly*.

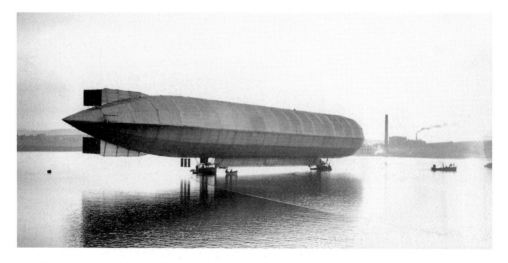

33 *His Majesty's Airship No.1*. Built for the navy by Vickers at Cavendish Dock, Barrow-in-Furness, it was popularly called *Mayfly*. It never flew. On 29 September 1911 it broke in two while being moved out of the shed.

The construction shed, not completed until 1910, was built on piles in the Cavendish Dock at Barrow-in-Furness so that the airship and gondola could, on completion, float inside the shed. In February 1911 trials of the airship were made in the shed, and members of the Advisory Committee for Aeronautics paid a visit to the site, where they were met by Captain Murray Sueter.

Three months after this, *HMA No.1* was moved out of the shed for engine trials. (It took 300 sailors an hour to get the airship out.) A few days later it was damaged on the shed door. On 29 September 1911 the airship was being towed out of the shed, stern first, by a steam launch. *HMA No.1* heeled over, and a bulge was seen in the centre; the bow went up, and the rear part sank into the water, endangering Lieutenants Talbot and Usborne, who were in the gondola. Britain's first rigid airship had practically broken in two, and it was eventually returned to the shed – where it stayed.

Naval Airship No.2 was the former *Willows No.4*, but it made only a few flights as a naval airship.

Naval Airship No.3/Astra-Torres: This French airship, with its bright yellow envelope, was delivered to Farnborough in the spring of 1913. On a flight on 12 June 1913 the two French pilots were accompanied by Commander Masterman, Lieutenant Usborne, Major Maitland and some mechanics. They ascended to 2,000ft before a mechanical fault developed and the airship returned to earth on Farnborough Common. The *Astra-Torres* was then subjected to a series of mooring trials: the mooring places looked like megaphones fixed at the top of high poles. The airship's 'nose' went into one of these, where it was fastened, and could then swing around with the wind, like a ship at moorings.

In late September the airship achieved a record 51.1mph, before being handed over to the Royal Navy.

Naval Airship No.4/Parseval PL18: The Parseval was accepted by the Admiralty in May 1913, and arrived from Germany a few weeks later. It could fly at over 40mph, with its two 180hp Maybach engines driving two four-bladed propellers. It was 275ft long x 49ft diameter, with a capacity of 310,640 cubic feet. The envelope was made of Metzeler ballonstoff, treated with aluminium.

34 *Naval Airship No.3/Astra-Torres.* This French airship was delivered to Farnborough in the spring of 1913. In September of that year it achieved a top speed of over 50mph.

UNITED STATES

CHARLES FRANCIS RITCHEL

A dirigible flight was made at Hartford, Connecticut, on 12 June 1878, in a machine designed by Charles F. Ritchel of Bridgeport, Connecticut. The craft had flown before, at the 1876 Centennial Exhibition in Philadelphia, carrying Mabel Harrington and Mark Quinlan, but that was indoors. The cylindrical envelope was made by Goodyear, and underneath was a brass framework on which sat the aeronaut, turning a small propeller by muscle-power.

The Hartford flight was made by Mark Quinlan, who took off from a baseball field, passed over the tall brick buildings of the Colt firearms factory, over the Connecticut River, and back to the start. A few more ascents were made, in Boston and elsewhere, but the machine had the disadvantages of being dependent on the power of one (light-weight) person for propulsion, and of needing flat, calm weather.

THOMAS SCOTT BALDWIN (1854–1923)

T.S. Baldwin was born in 1854. His parents died when he was twelve, and two years later he joined a circus, working as an acrobat. He first went up in a balloon in 1875 and began touring, with his brother, as 'Captain Tom', performing on a trapeze underneath a hot-air balloon (he was not the only one to do this – L.G. Mecklem of Seattle was another, for example).

35 The flying machine of Charles F. Ritchel, as shown on the cover of *Harper's Weekly* of 13 July 1878. It had flown, a month earlier, at Hartford, Connecticut.

For a decade the brothers took their act to county fairs in the United States, and to Canada and the Far East. They then decided to develop a new act, involving parachuting from a balloon. Captain Tom's first public showing of this was at San Francisco, the second at Quincy, Illinois, and the third took place on 9 August 1887, at Rockaway Beach, New York, before 20,000 spectators. The balloon, filled with hydrogen, was 'in color and in shape like an abnormal Bartlett pear with the stem down'. For his jump Captain Tom was dressed in 'pink tights and blue bespangled trunks, with his feet encased in a heavy pair of shoes'.

After ten years of this kind of activity, Baldwin cast around for a new attraction, hit on the idea of dirigible flight and in 1898 (the year of the first flight of the *Santos Dumont No.1*) went to France on a 'fact-finding' trip. Baldwin's own airship made its first test flight on 29 July 1904, and was demonstrated in public five days later at Oakland, California. The *California Arrow* was a small non-rigid, 52ft long x 17ft diameter, with an 8,000 cubic feet capacity. Below the envelope, which was made of Japanese silk, hung a wooden framework which carried the 10hp Curtiss engine; the rudder was at the back and the propeller, at the front, could be reversed for manoeuvring. Ascent and descent were controlled by the aeronaut changing his position on the framework.

At the end of October 1904 the *California Arrow* created a sensation at the Louisiana Purchase Exposition, popularly known as the World's Fair, at St Louis. The whole site covered 1,200 acres; 1,500 buildings had been erected and sixty-three countries provided exhibits. Twelve acres, surrounded by a high fence, were allocated for aeronautical activities, for which there were large cash prizes. Newspaper headlines read: 'Baldwin's Airship Makes a Successful Flight. Navigator manoeuvres at will above World's Fair grounds.' A dispatch from St Louis, dated 31 October 1904, informed readers that 'After circling in every direction at a height of 2,000ft above the Cascades, in sight of cheering, enthusiastic spectators on the World's Fair grounds, A. Roy Knabenshue of Toledo, in command of Thomas Baldwin's airship *California Arrow*, today returned to the place from which he started, covering three and a half miles, part way against an eight-mile wind' (*New York Times*, 1 November 1904). A second flight, of thirty-six minutes, was made on the following day 'amid cheering thousands'.

On Christmas Day 1904 Knabenshue showed off the *California Arrow* in Los Angeles, taking off from the Chutes Park baseball ground and flying for over an hour.

36 A. Roy Knabenshue with T.S. Baldwin's *California Arrow* at the St Louis World's Fair in October 1904.

Baldwin went on to provide airship displays in many places, and was contracted to appear at the Lewis and Clark Centennial Exposition at Portland, Oregon. Open from 1 June 1905 to mid-October 1905, 1.5 million people paid to be admitted to the 400-acre site on the shores of Guild's Lake. Charles Knox, developer of granulated gelatine, had arranged for the word *Gelatine* to be displayed prominently on the envelope of Baldwin's airship.

The United States Army began to take notice of dirigibles. The Army Signal Corps formed an aeronautical division on 1 August 1907, which was 'to take charge of all matters pertaining to military ballooning, air machines and all kindred subjects'. They were interested in Baldwin's airship, but wanted it to be able to lift a heavier load, have a stronger envelope, and to be able to stay in the air for longer. An improved Baldwin dirigible was sent for trials at Fort Myer in August 1908. It was 90ft long x 20ft diameter, with an envelope of two layers of silk with one of rubber between. Air was blown into a ballonet by blowers worked by hand or motor. The wooden framework was braced with wire, and carried a new 20hp Curtiss engine. It was described as 'the great grey torpedo, with its flimsy substructure bearing a noisy motor and two passengers at either end.' The airship was bought by the army, designated *Signal Corps Airship No.1* (*SC-1*), and used for training at Fort Omaha, Nebraska. A month after the trials of Baldwin's airship, Fort Myer saw another test flight, when Orville Wright demonstrated the new *Wright Flyer* (Model A) aeroplane.

THOMAS CHALKLEY BENBOW

T.C. Benbow formed the American Aerial Navigation Company at Red Lodge, Montana, in 1902. The first trial of the *Meteor* in April 1902 was unsuccessful because of the 'inferior and limited supply of gas', and it was announced that another envelope would be made at the 'balloon farm' of Carl Myers at Frankfort, New York. The *Meteor* was taken to St Louis to compete at the 1904 World's Fair where it made three tethered ascents and towards the end of November was in the air for forty-five minutes, but it was dirigible for only a short period.

In the following year Benbow found chrome deposits in the Beartooth Mountains, south of Columbus, Ohio, and spent the rest of his life in the mining business.

CHARLES F. STROBEL

From about 1905 a number of small airships began to appear, performing for crowds at 'expositions' and on the county fair circuit. Prominent among the providers of this kind of aeronautical entertainment was Charles F. Strobel, manager of the Toledo Mud Hens baseball team from 1896 to 1902. He worked with A. Roy Knabenshue in producing such shows, and in 1906 formed the Strobel Dirigible Company. Strobel did not himself fly, but provided airships and pilots to tour the country. Lincoln Beachey and Roy Knabenshue flew Strobel airships, and others employed included Harry Ginders, Frank Goodale, C.O. Jones, E.J. Parker and Stanley Vaughan.

In 1907 two Strobel airships – flown by Lincoln Beachey and Jack Dallas – won the first and second prizes in a competition organised by the Aero Club of St Louis 'for the longest and best continuous flight'. T.S. Baldwin came in third. Charles Oliver Jones made his first ascent (in the Strobel *Boomerang*: 25,000 cubic feet, 105ft long x 24ft diameter) on 17 June 1908. Within three months he was dead: the airship caught fire in flight over the fair grounds at Waterlooville, Missouri.

SOUVENIR

KANSAS STATE FAIR,
HUTCHINSON, KANS.
SEPT. 14-19, 1908.

37 One of Charles F. Strobel's airships at the Kansas State Fair in September 1908. Strobel's
dirigibles appeared at expositions and county fairs throughout the United States.

1910 was a busy year. In February three Strobel airships were sent to the Great Panama
Canal Exposition at Tampa, Florida, with pilots Evan J. Parker, Frank Goodale and Stanley
Vaughan. Parker had gone to Toledo to work on the construction of Strobel's dirigibles,
and first took charge of an airship flight on 31 August 1908, at Hutchinson, during the
Kansas State Fair. Goodale, born at Bowling Green, Ohio, was nineteen years old. Vaughan,
aged twenty-three, had piloted for the first time a year earlier.

Strobel dirigibles gave displays in June 1910 at Chartiers City, Pennsylvania; in July at
Manchester (New Hampshire); in Massachusetts at Lawrence, Lowell, Lynn, Brockton
and Fall River, and at Salisbury, Maryland. In September at McKee's Rock, Pennsylvania
and Knoxville, Tennessee. At Topeka, Kansas, the rudder broke during a flight by Harry
Ginders and 'the airship whirled round and round, stood at angles near the perpendicular,
first on one end and then on the other, but finally was landed safely.' Palisades Amusement
Park, New Jersey, advertised flights by 'the world's youngest boy aeronaut, Frank Goodale'.
Bookings in October included Columbus, Mississippi and San Antonio, Texas. In the
winter Strobel sent Parker and Goodale to Puerto Rico, to give a display at San Juan.

In June 1911 Frank Goodale made 'his third annual night trip' to *The Times* building from
the Palisades Amusement Park, New Jersey. Flying low along Broadway he was cheered on
by thousands in the streets and on rooftops.

The impresario behind all these airship displays, Charles F. Strobel, died of typhoid in
1915 at the age of fifty-one.

A. ROY KNABENSHUE (1876–1960)

Augustus Roy Knabenshue was born at Lancaster, Ohio, where his father Samuel was
superintendent of schools for two years, before becoming night editor of the *Ohio State
Journal*. The family moved to Toledo in 1883, and the following year Samuel joined the
Toledo Blade as chief editorial writer.

Roy acquired a balloon in 1899 and took it to fairs where, as 'Professor Carlos', he allowed paying customers to ascend (it was tethered). His ballooning activities took him to the 1904 St Louis World's Fair, where he met Thomas S. Baldwin, who asked him to pilot his *California Arrow* (see page 65).

The next year was to be a full one for Roy Knabenshue. In January 1905 he raced the *California Arrow* against a Pope-Toledo motor car from Curtis Park, Los Angeles, to the Raymond Hotel in Pasadena, winning by two minutes. Returning to his home town of Toledo, Knabenshue flew Strobel's exhibition airships, and decided to build one of his own – *Toledo I*. The display program of his new craft was managed by Charles F. Strobel.

Adelbert Spitzer had announced a $500 prize for the first person to land on the top of his ten-storey building in Toledo, a feat which Roy Knabenshue achieved on his airship's first outing on 28 June 1905. A month later he took his *Toledo II* (7,000 cubic feet; 62ft long x 16ft diameter) to New York, where he stopped the traffic by flying over the city on 20 August. He flew around *The Times* building, and was in the air for an hour and forty-three minutes, giving the city its first sight of a dirigible.

Before the end of the month Roy Knabenshue was in the air over Chicago: a first attempt ended in a crash, but on 27 August he flew from 63rd Street to 46th Street and back, watched by 'an immense throng'. In October 1905 *Toledo 2* arrived by train (with Knabenshue and Strobel) at Brockton, Massachusetts. The flight was not a success – the engine stopped and the craft hit a flagpole. Knabenshue came back in 1906 – on a no fly, no fee basis – and *Toledo* performed perfectly.

In August 1906 Lincoln Beachey flew over Washington in Knabenshue's airship. Starting from Luna Park, he went round the Washington Monument before descending near the White House. The press reported that 'Business at the White House, in the Treasury and in the State, War and Navy department buildings were practically forced to halt. Clerks, employees and even high officials dropped everything and rushed to windows and doors

FIRST SUCCESSFUL FLIGHT OF AIR SHIP, KNABENSHUE, KING OF THE AIR, IN FLIGHT
FROM FAIR GROUNDS TO THE TOP OF THE SPITZER BLDG. JUNE 28, 1905, TOLEDO, O.

38 A. Roy Knabenshue's *Toledo I*. On its first flight, in June 1905, Knabenshue won the $500 prize offered by Adelbert Spitzer to the first person to land on top of his ten-storey building in Toledo.

to see a real airship in operation.' Beachey then flew over the Capitol, where both houses were in session.

Roy Knabenshue's closest call came on 8 June 1907 at Hartford, Connecticut, where he was making daily flights. The airship lost height rapidly, and crashed into the river, where the aeronaut became tangled up in the debris. He managed to struggle clear and was pulled out of the water.

Knabenshue was back in his home town in May 1908. Flying in a strong breeze, his airship was damaged when the engine failed and he crashed on to a baseball ground, interrupting Toledo's match with Indianapolis. The airship was flying again a fortnight later. By 1909 he and the young Lincoln Beachey were co-operating in providing displays, and in January 1910 they attended the First International Aviation Meet, at Dominguez Field, Los Angeles. The star performers were Louis Paulhan, with his Bleriot monoplane and Farman biplane, and Roy Knabenshue in his airship. Lieutenant Beck, an officer of the US Army Signal Corps, flew with Knabenshue, reconnoitring simulated enemy positions and troop movements, taking aerial photographs, and trying to hit targets on the ground with bags of sand.

Two months later Knabenshue was asked to become manager of the Wright brothers' aeroplane exhibition team, but the Wrights disbanded it in November 1911 and Roy Knabenshue returned to dirigibles. By the summer of 1913 his new airship, designed to carry thirteen passengers, was nearing completion at Pasadena. Its capacity was 75,231 cubic feet, and it was 150ft long x 30ft diameter. The first flight of *Pasadena* was in September 1913 and for a short period it was employed carrying passengers between Pasadena, Los Angeles, Santa Monica and Long Beach. The service could not be sustained and Knabenshue's airship was hired by Chicago's White City Amusement Park, where – renamed *White City* – it flew for a month in the summer of 1914.

JOHN A. MORRELL

The National Airship Company was founded by John A. Morrell in 1906, with the object of building a large passenger-carrying dirigible. He announced that the new airship would be 360ft long x 32ft diameter, and capable of transporting seven crew and twenty passengers. Morrell declared that: 'Aerial navigation is solved' and before the middle of the next year he 'would be dispensing tickets for airship tours from San Francisco to New York in 24 hours.'

Two years later Morrell was promising that a fleet of airships would be operating within three months. This promise was made at the same time as a large number of stockholders were demanding an official investigation into the affairs of the National Airship Company.

The airship built for Morrell was 450ft long x 46ft maximum diameter, and was described as being cigar-shaped, with 'aeroplane rudders and wings'. The power was provided by five 50hp engines, which were attached to a keel under the envelope. Each engine was attended by its own engineer, who sat next to it.

The ascent at Berkeley, California, was made on 23 May 1908 before a crowd of 10,000, and proceeded in spite of the warnings of experienced balloonists, who believed that the airship was unsafe. Fyodor A. Postnikov (formerly a Russian army engineer, but a Berkeley resident since 1906) thought that the envelope's fabric was not strong enough, and advised against the flight.

The ascent began, but the nose of the airship kept tipping upwards, putting the passengers in fear of being ejected. Then there was the sound of tearing, a gas bag burst, and the airship fell to the ground. The pilot, John Byrne, was seen to be clinging to the netting of the envelope; when he regained consciousness after the crash he said:

39 The *Morrell* airship at Berkeley, California, on 23 May 1908. It was 450ft long x 40ft maximum diameter and was powered by five engines. Morrell was warned that his airship was unsafe, but went ahead anyway.

> I am not much hurt. I got to the topmost point of the balloon before we struck the ground. I was climbing up the bag when I heard a pouf. And the smell of gas came to my nostrils. I turned my head and climbed away from it. I knew if I got below the bag I might be crushed to death by the machinery, so I climbed on, and when we hit I had the bag under me.

All those on board survived, although sustaining broken limbs and bruises. 'Captain Penfold – the Australian aeronaut' (real name, Vincent Patrick Taylor) was one of the passengers:

> The ascension was a good one, but soon after we were up one end of the bag began to tip. I looked at Morrell and saw him make his way through the machinery to the higher end. He cried: 'This way, boys.' His idea was to weigh down that end and thus allow us to go down evenly. At that time the machine was going down without a rush. I tried to follow him but before I knew it the machine hit the ground. I watched the heavy machinery above me and dodged it. I blame nobody. I took the consequences by going in the ascension after Morrell had told me not to. I want to say that Morrell kept his head throughout the entire occurrence.

Within a month John Morrell had been charged with embezzlement, and was said to have 'fraudulently represented himself as an inventor of national prominence'. Alexander Otts (superintendent of construction for Morrell, and also a stockholder) further charged that the airship crash was the result of 'deliberate and premeditated design on the part of the said Morrell, to prevent an ascension, despite his apparent efforts to the contrary.' Otts

40 The crash of the *Morrell* airship on 23 May 1908 at Berkeley. Incredibly, no one was killed.

stated that John Morrell 'well knew that the said airship as constructed could not be successfully operated, and made the said ascension for the sole purpose of keeping alive the hopes of stockholders of the said National Airship Company to further his own ends.'

In July it was decided that Morrell and fourteen others would be put on trial. At the end of September the *Oakland Tribune* reported that, following the issue of a warrant for his arrest, Morrell had disappeared. Alexander Otts was sure that he had left the country.

WALTER WELLMAN (1858–1935)

Walter Wellman and his brother Frank founded the *Penny Paper* at Cincinatti in 1881. They sold it two years later, when Walter went to Chicago as the political correspondent of the *Chicago Herald*, which later became the *Record-Herald*. In 1892 he was sent by his newspaper to determine where Columbus had made his landfall 400 years before. Wellman concluded that it had been on Watling Island in the Bahamas.

Walter Wellman then turned his attention to the Arctic, making what he called 'a summer dash for the pole' – which took three months – in 1894. Four years later, on 26 June 1898, another Wellman expedition – four Americans and five Norwegians – assembled at Tromsø for another attempt to reach the North Pole, via Franz Josef Land. They hoped, also, to find some trace of Salomon Andrée, Knut Fraenkel and Nils Srindberg, who had disappeared on their Arctic balloon flight of 1897. Wellman's expedition had no success.

Weary of dogs, foot-slogging, and falling into crevasses, Walter Wellman decided to fly
to the North Pole by making the first airship journey in the Arctic. He raised a quarter
of a million dollars for his *Wellman Chicago Record-Herald Polar Expedition*, which would
be based on the island of Danskøya, in the Svalbard archipeligo, about 620 miles from the
geographical Pole. An advance party led by Henry B. Hersey, of the US Weather Bureau,
reached Danskøya on 21 June 1906. With him on the steamer *Frithjof* were seventeen men,
and the materials to erect a gas plant, workshop, living quarters and a 'balloon house'. The
Frithjof had to make three round trips to Tromso. The camp contained, as well as forty
men:

> half a ship-load of provisions; the aeronautic machine and all its appurtenances: dog-sledges,
> motor-sledges, a steam boiler and engine, tons of gasoline, tools, coal, iron rods, bolts, nails,
> steel boats, and all the paraphernalia of what a London periodical aptly termed 'Mr Wellman's
> scientific village in the Arctic'. (Wellman, 1911).

The hangar for the airship was built by Alexandre Liwentaal, who had worked for
Lachambre, Lebaudy and Zeppelin; covered in canvas, it was 200ft high x 85ft wide x 85ft
high.

On 8 July 1906 the crated dirigible arrived at Spitzbergen. The non-rigid *America*, built
in Paris at the workshop of Mutin Louis Godard, was 164ft long x 52ft diameter, and
224,240 cubic feet capacity. A ballonet was inflated by a blower, powered by a 5hp engine.
Two engines – one of 50hp and one of 25hp – drove two propellers. The airship was found
to be unsatisfactory and was sent back to Paris, where a new engine was fitted and the
envelope's capacity increased.

Wellman's expedition was back at Spitzbergen by June of the next year. The attempt
to fly to the Pole began on 2 September 1907 – on board were Walter Wellman (in command), Melvin Vaniman (engines) and Felix Reisenberg (navigation). The *America* ascended
– handled by a ground crew of forty – and a steel cable was lowered to the steamer *Express*,
which was to tow the airship out to sea. After about half an hour's free flight, it was found
that the compass was not working, and that the weather had deteriorated. The engines
were stopped, and the crew managed to bring the *America* down on to a glacier. They had
been in the air for just over two hours.

The *Express* steamed up near to the face of the glacier, and the rescuers, roped together,
made their way over the ice. The aeronauts and the airship, which had suffered little
damage, were transported back to base, and Wellman's 'scientific village' was made ready to
withstand a winter.

In April 1909 *America* was brought from Paris to occupy a prominent place at the
Aeronautical and Motor Boat Exhibition at Olympia, London, before being transported to
Spitzbergen for another attempt on the Pole. It was found that one of the three men left at
Camp Wellman had died, and the balloon shed had been wrecked by a storm. This second
flight for the Pole also failed: in August 1909 the rebuilt *America* flew (with Wellman,
Vaniman, Vaniman's brother-in-law Louis Loud, and Russian balloonist Nikolai Popov)
for about thirty miles before the guide rope was torn away. This guide rope – known as
the 'equilibrator', and devised by Wellman – was a tube 6in in diameter, made of leather
an inch thick. It was divided internally into sections of about 10ft, in which were carried
emergency provisions. To prevent damage to the leather its outer surface was covered with
thousands of thin, riveted, steel plates. When the guide rope fell away the airship, relieved
of this weight, shot upwards, until it was brought under control and pointed to the south,
trying to make headway against strong winds. The steamer *Fram* was able to take a tow

41 Walter Wellman planned to fly to the North Pole in his dirigible *America*. Based at Spitzbergen, he mounted expeditions with this airship in 1906, 1907 and 1909, but without success.

rope, but the strain was too great, and the *America* had to put down on the surface of the sea. The airship was towed back to Virgo Bay, and the expedition abandoned.

The longest flight by an airship up to this time had been made over Germany a year earlier — 360 miles by the rigid Zeppelin *LZ4* before it crashed at Echterdingen. A successful flight over the North Pole by the non-rigid *America* would have involved a return journey of 1,400 miles, in conditions not previously experienced by an airship, with no chance of replenishing stocks of food or fuel, and little chance of rescue in an emergency.

In September 1909 Frederick A. Cooke and Robert E. Peary announced that they had, separately, reached the Pole. Walter Wellman now turned his back on the idea of flying to the North Pole and decided, instead, to make the first aerial crossing of the North Atlantic. He was aware of German plans for an Atlantic flight, and he intended to set off in 1910.

The venture was supported by the *New York Times*, the *Chicago Record-Herald* and the London *Daily Telegraph*. To house the airship the Aero Club of Atlantic City erected a shed 250ft long x 80ft wide x 80ft high, and a hydrogen-making plant was brought from Paris. It needed eighty tons of sulphuric acid and sixty tons of iron filings.

The *America* had been modified and renovated, and was now 228ft long x 52ft diameter, with a capacity of 345,000 cubic feet. The steel gondola was 156ft long. As in the Arctic the long, hollow equilibrator was attached, dangling 300ft below and containing twenty-nine fuel tanks. A lifeboat with Marconi wireless installed was slung about 6ft below the gondola, with a connecting rope ladder.

A month before his departure date, Walter Wellman gave his views on the future of airships in an after-dinner speech in Atlantic City:

We believe that the airship will do more than any other single agency to bring about universal peace. War is barbaric, and should be made obsolete. The way to make war impossible is to make it so destructive that all the world will at once see that it is suicide and crime to go to war. Vaniman and I believe that we know how to adapt airships to warfare in such a manner as to make armed conflict almost inconceivably terrible and ruinous. If we are right, a fleet of ten airships could not only destroy battleships, naval stations, fortresses, camps, bridges, arsenals and strategic points, but could lay waste cities, strike terror to scores and millions of people, and overawe the most courageous and resourceful nation … If my friend Andrew Carnegie, who has already done so much good in the world, wants to bring about universal peace, let him endow with a million or two a plant for aerial development.

Criticism of the proposed Atlantic venture had not been absent: Wellman's airship was described as a 'worn-out gas-bag' with an 'old coffee mill' of an engine, and Wellman later referred to the 'calumny and abuse' he had to suffer. Delayed for a fortnight by the weather, the *America* finally ascended from Atlantic City at 8.00 a.m. on Saturday 15 October 1910. No trial flight had been made. On board were Walter Wellman, Melvin Vaniman (chief engineer), Louis Loud (1st assistant engineer), John Aubert (2nd assistant engineer), Jack Kirby (wireless operator, from West Australia), and Murray Simon (the British navigator, on leave from the White Star Liner *Oceanic*). The cat from the airship shed accompanied them.

For the first fifteen minutes the *America* was towed by a launch carrying reporters from the sponsoring newspapers. At some point three of the equilibrator's fuel tanks were punctured, and the cat was now rushing around and being a nuisance in the gondola. An attempt was made to lower the animal in a canvas bag to the press boat, but the water was too rough, the animal was hauled back up, and subsequently behaved itself.

At 10.50 a.m. a wireless message was sent to the *New York Times*: 'Airship *America*, of Atlantic City – Good start. Everything working well, and have fresh north winds. Fog still thick. – Wellman.' By early the next morning the airship was in trouble – it was losing gas and the engines had broken down, turning it into a free balloon. In the afternoon it was realised that an Atlantic crossing was out of the question, and Loud and Aubert began dismantling the heaviest engine, so that it could be dropped into the sea. Jack Kirby sent off a CQD message – the Marconi distress call: 'Its all up. Arranging to take to boat. Serious problem. Calling CQD.'

The crew now spent most of their time in the lifeboat, which carried stocks of food and water as well as the wireless gear. To keep the airship in the air anything moveable had been jettisoned, but *America* was now only about 50ft above the water. They were 350 miles from Cape Hatteras, North Carolina. At about 5.00 a.m. a vessel was sighted – the British steamship *Trent*, on passage from Bermuda to New York. Messages were exchanged by lamp, and then by wireless. Three hours later all the aviators, including the cat, were safely on board the *Trent*.

The *America*'s crew arrived at Atlantic City by rail, and were escorted from the station to the Hotel Chalfonte by a detachment of soldiers and a band. There was a dinner, followed by speeches. A. T. Bell, the secretary of the Wellman syndicate, said:

Atlantic City is proud of Walter Wellman and his men and of those who made his attempt possible. We should not forget those who braved criticism in the financial backing of the Wellman project. We hope that the attempt to reach Europe through the air will not stop with the trip just ended.

42 The Wellman airship *America* seen from the British steamship *Trent*, after the failed attempt to fly across the Atlantic.

43 Melvin Vaniman's *Akron* at Atlantic City on 2 July 1912 preparing to leave on a test flight. Twenty minutes into the flight the craft exploded, killing Vaniman and the four crew members.

Walter Wellman, then aged fifty-two, decided to stick to journalism and lived another twenty-five years.

MELVIN VANIMAN (1866–1912)

Chester Melvin Vaniman, born in 1866, was brought up on the farm of his parents, George and Louisa, near Virden, Macoupin County, Illinois. After attending the Mount Pleasant College (run by the German Baptist Brethren) he toured for some years with an opera company, photographing the places he visited. Around 1900, in Hawaii, Melvin Vaniman left the company and became a professional freelance photographer – he designed and made a camera for taking 'panoramic' pictures, using it in Hawaii, New Zealand and Australia. He then decided to try his luck in Europe, but his panoramas of cities were unsuccessful, because of the poorer light and weather.

Vaniman had some experience with balloons, using them to take photographs from a height, and he now took on a prominent role in Walter Wellman's attempts to reach the North Pole in 1907 and 1909, as well as his Atlantic debacle of 1910. Wellman gave up on airships after this, but Vaniman decided to have another go at crossing the Atlantic.

The project was financed by Frank A. Seibling, founder of the Goodyear Tire and Rubber Company, which made the dirigible's envelope. Completed in the autumn of 1911, the *Akron* was 258ft long x 47ft diameter; 400,000 cubic feet capacity. Beneath the envelope was a tank for 8,000 gallons of petrol, which formed the keel. Underneath that was slung a lifeboat with stores for twenty days, and wireless equipment supplied by Marconi.

Vaniman's airship was housed in a shed near Absecon Inlet, Atlantic City. The first trial, on 5 November 1911, ended after an hour, with *Akron* sitting on the mud flats of Grassy Bay, waiting to be towed home.

A trial flight was scheduled for 2 July 1912. At 6.20 a.m. the handling crew of fire-men and policemen let go of the ropes, and the cream-coloured craft, watched by about 3,000 people, rose into the air. On board were Melvin Vaniman, his brother Calvin, George Bourtillon, Fred Elmer and Walter Guest. After a flight of about twenty minutes, *Akron* exploded and the wreckage dropped straight down into the sea. All were killed.

III

AIRSHIPS AT WAR
1914–1918

GERMAN MILITARY AIRSHIPS

The First World War began when Germany declared war on France and, on 4 August 1914, invaded Belgium. On the night of 5/6 August German Army Zeppelin *ZVI* bombed Liège, killing nine people.

The German Army went into the war with six Zeppelin airships and one Schütte-Lanz, but four were lost in the first month: *ZV* at the Battle of Tannenberg; *ZVI* was badly damaged whilst bombing Liège; *ZVII* was shot down in Alsace; and *ZVIII* was forced down at Badonvillers. In October *ZIX* was bombed and destroyed in its shed at Düsseldorf by an aeroplane of the British Royal Naval Air Service, which had flown the hundred miles from Antwerp.

Twenty-eight more airships were to enter service with the army – in 1914, three Zeppelins; 1915, nine Zeppelins and two Schütte-Lanz; 1916, nine Zeppelins and three Schütte-Lanz; 1917, two Zeppelins.

Apart from joining in the attacks on the British Isles, German Army airships were in action at places such as Warsaw, Bucharest and Brest-Litovsk, as well as at Odessa and Mudros. Bombing and reconnaissance sorties were flown over Belgium and northern France; bombs were dropped on Paris and Calais.

The German High Seas Fleet found itself lacking in reconnaissance capabilities. To build surface vessels to do the job would be very expensive, and take years. The aeroplanes of the time were incapable of fulfilling such a role, but airships could stay aloft for long periods, could hover, and could carry heavy wireless equipment. They were faster than surface vessels, cheaper to build and operate, could patrol a larger sea area, and could be brought into service quickly. Considerations such as these led to the expansion of the Naval Airship Division. In 1914 the navy had six airships in commission. In 1915 there were twelve new Zeppelins and three Schütte-Lanz; in 1916, a dozen Zeppelins went into service with the navy, and four Schütte-Lanz; in 1917, sixteen Zeppelins and one Schütte-Lanz.

The size of the navy dirigibles increased over the war years: *L1* to *L8* (commissioned October 1912 to December 1914) were just over 500ft long, and of about 795,000 cubic feet capacity. *L10* to *L24* (May 1915 to May 1916) were 540–580ft long; 1,264,000 cubic feet. *L30* to *L56* (July 1916 to September 1917) were around 650ft long, and of almost 2,000,000 cubic feet. *L57, L59, L70* and *L71* (September 1917 to July 1918) had a capacity of over 2,000,000 cubic feet.

Zeppelins were built at Friedrichshafen, Löwenthal, Potsdam and Staaken, with engines made at Friedrichshafen by Maybach, and gas cells at Tempelhof. The home of Schütte-Lanz was Mannheim, with some craft built at Leipzig. The Parseval Company was at Bitterfeld.

GERMAN AIR RAIDS ON BRITAIN

1915

The first airship raid on Britain was carried out on 19/20 January 1915 by naval airships based at Fühlsbüttel (Hamburg) and Nordholz (near Cuxhafen). The target of *L6* was London, but engine failure caused the airship to return to base. *L3* and *L4* were making for the Humber, but ended up bombing Norfolk. This was typical of many sorties – navigation was often difficult and the intended targets were not hit.

L3 arrived first and passed over Great Yarmouth at about 8.20 p.m., dropping thirteen bombs in ten minutes, and killing two people. Two of the unexploded bombs were later exhibited at the Drill Hall, when they were described as being pear-shaped, about 30in long, and weighing 110lb.

The captain of *L4* thought that he was north of the Humber when he was in reality over north Norfolk, eighty miles away. His first missiles fell on Sheringham. King's Lynn received hits on an engine-house at the docks and a nearby dwelling. Three cottages were destroyed in Bentinck Street, killing two people.

On 31 May 1915 the army's *LZ38* (commanded by Erich Linnarz) came in over Margate and Southend to become the first airship to drop bombs on London, at just before 11.00 p.m. Seven Londoners died and thirty-three were injured. The official communiqué from Berlin announced that 'as a reprisal for the bombardment of the open town of Lüdwigshafen, we last night threw numerous bombs on the wharves and docks of London' – not, in fact, on the docks, but on the north-eastern part of the city. (Four days before, eighteen French aeroplanes had attacked the chemical factory at Lüdwifgshafen, a raid which was described as retaliation for an air raid on Paris.)

Flight Sub-Lieutenant Reginald Warneford won his Victoria Cross near Ghent on the night of 4/5 June 1915 when he destroyed the German Army's *LZ37*, in flight, by dropping bombs on it. The explosion turned his aircraft over, and his engine stopped, forcing Warneford to land behind enemy lines. He was able to restart the engine and returned to base. Reginald Warneford was killed less than a fortnight later, on a test flight in a Farman F27 aeroplane.

London was again targeted on the night of 13/14 October 1915. Naval airships *L11*, *L14* and *L15* set off from Nordholz, and *L13* and *L16* from Hage. Bombs were dropped on Croydon, Hertford (where *L16* killed nine and injured fifteen), Hythe, Tunbridge Wells and Woolwich. Joachim Breithaupt in *L15* was the only commander to reach central London, hitting an area north of the Strand. In Wellington Street seventeen people died. Bombs fell near the Strand Theatre, the Waldorf Hotel and the Inns of Court. In the whole attack seventy-one people were killed and 130 injured.

In addition to the raids described above, during the year 1915 bombs fell on Tyneside, Lowestoft, Maldon, Bury St Edmunds, Southend, Ramsgate, Gravesend, Hull, Goole, Dover, Harwich, Ashford and Croydon. In all, twenty raids killed over 200 people in the year and injured 533.

1916

A fleet of nine naval airships set off to bomb Liverpool on 31 January 1916. After crossing the English coastline near the Wash, none was able to find their objective, although some

THE ZEPPELIN SINKING IN THE THAMES ESTUARY, SATURDAY, APRIL 1ST, 1916.
DAILY SKETCH PHOTOGRAPH

44 Naval Zeppelin *L15* shot down on 1 April 1916 near Margate. One man died and seventeen were taken prisoner.

crews thought they had. Burton-on-Trent (about eighty miles from Liverpool) was worst hit – three airships dropped over 200 high-explosive bombs and 170 incendiaries in the early hours of the morning, leaving seventy people dead and 113 injured. Other raids were made on Derby, Dudley, Tipton and Wednesbury. The whole sortie killed seventy (twenty-nine men, twenty-six women and fifteen children) and injured 113 (forty-four men, fifty women and nineteen children). On its return journey, *L19* (Captain: Odo Loewe) had to ditch in the North Sea, where the Zeppelin was sighted by the trawler *King Stephen*. The airship's crew of fifteen outnumbered that of the trawler, and the boat's skipper feared that his vessel would be hijacked if he took them on board, so he left the scene. *L19*'s crew all drowned.

Two months after this attack on the Midlands, London was the target for a flotilla of seven navy and three army airships. Four of them turned back because of the weather or engine trouble. *L15* (Captain: Joachim Breithaupt), shot down by anti-aircraft fire on 1 April 1916, crashed in the sea off Margate. One man died and the rest (seventeen) were captured.

The biggest raid on Britain came on the night of 2/3 September 1916, carried out by twelve naval and four army airships (although one naval and one army craft turned back). At about 2.00 a.m. the army's Schütte-Lanz *SL11* (Captain: Wilhelm Schramm) was caught by a searchlight, and was then chased by twenty-one-years-old Lieutenant William Leefe Robinson in his BE2c; he shot it down in flames using the new incendiary ammunition, killing sixteen men. Robinson's victims fell at Cuffley, Hertfordshire, where thousands of people turned up to see the wreckage. The Germans were buried with military honours at Potters Bar, and Robinson was awarded the Victoria Cross.

In the raid as a whole, the Germans had dropped more than 500 bombs, many jettisoned by commanders anxious to depart after seeing the fate of *SL11*. Four people were killed and sixteen injured.

Three weeks later another airship was shot down, this time by anti-aircraft fire. *L33* (Captain: Alois Böcker), part of a raid by twelve airships, had released bombs on London's East End before being hit. The Zeppelin came down in a field at New Hall Farm, Little

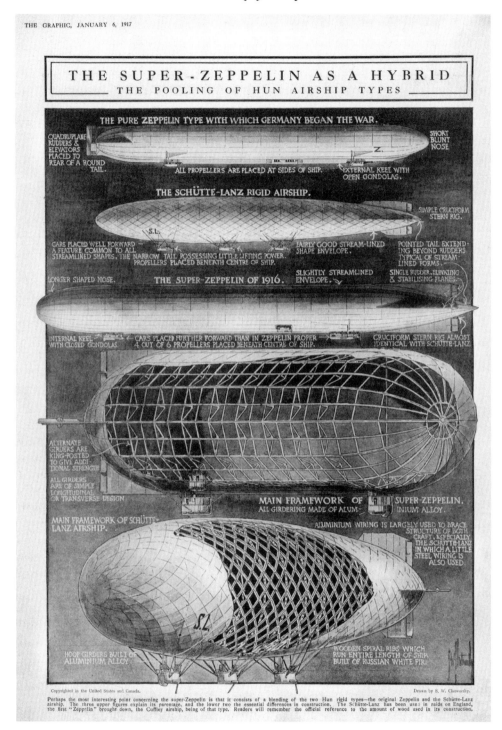

THE GRAPHIC, JANUARY 6, 1917

THE SUPER-ZEPPELIN AS A HYBRID

THE POOLING OF HUN AIRSHIP TYPES

THE PURE ZEPPELIN TYPE WITH WHICH GERMANY BEGAN THE WAR.

QUADRUPLANE RUDDERS & ELEVATORS PLACED TO REAR OF A ROUND TAIL.

SHORT BLUNT NOSE

ALL PROPELLERS ARE PLACED AT SIDES OF SHIP.

EXTERNAL KEEL WITH OPEN GONDOLAS.

THE SCHÜTTE-LANZ RIGID AIRSHIP.

SIMPLE CRUCIFORM STERN RIG.

CARS PLACED WELL FORWARD - A FEATURE COMMON TO ALL STREAMLINED SHAPES, THE NARROW TAIL POSSESSING LITTLE LIFTING POWER. PROPELLERS PLACED BENEATH CENTRE OF SHIP.

FAIRLY GOOD STREAM-LINED SHAPE ENVELOPE.

POINTED TAIL EXTEND-ING BEYOND RUDDERS TYPICAL OF STREAM-LINED FORMS.

LONGER SHAPED NOSE.

THE SUPER-ZEPPELIN OF 1916.

SLIGHTLY STREAMLINED ENVELOPE.

SINGLE RUDDER, ELEVATING & STABILISING PLANES.

INTERNAL KEEL WITH CLOSED GONDOLAS.

CARS PLACED FURTHER FORWARD THAN IN ZEPPELIN PROPER 4 OUT OF 6 PROPELLERS PLACED BENEATH CENTRE OF SHIP.

CRUCIFORM STERN RIG ALMOST IDENTICAL WITH SCHUTTE-LANZ

ALTERNATE GIRDERS ARE KING-POSTED TO GIVE ADDI-TIONAL STRENGTH

ALL GIRDERS ARE OF SIMPLE LONGITUDINAL OR TRANSVERSE DESIGN

MAIN FRAMEWORK OF SUPER-ZEPPELIN. ALL GIRDERING MADE OF ALUM-INIUM ALLOY.

MAIN FRAMEWORK OF SCHÜTTE-LANZ AIRSHIP.

ALUMINIUM WIRING IS LARGELY USED TO BRACE STRUCTURE OF BOTH CRAFT, ESPECIALLY THE SCHUTTE-LANZ IN WHICH A LITTLE STEEL WIRING IS ALSO USED.

HOOP GIRDERS BUILT OF ALUMINIUM ALLOY.

WOODEN SPIRAL RIBS WHICH RUN ENTIRE LENGTH OF SHIP BUILT OF RUSSIAN WHITE FIR.

Perhaps the most interesting point concerning the super-Zeppelin is that it consists of a blending of the two Hun rigid types—the original Zeppelin and the Schütte-Lanz airship. The three upper figures explain its parentage, and the lower two the essential differences in construction. The Schütte-Lanz has been used in raids on England, the first "Zeppelin" brought down, the Cuffley airship, being of that type. Readers will remember the official reference to the amount of wood used in its construction.

45 These drawings were published in *The Graphic* of 6 January 1917. The three upper drawings are of a Zeppelin, a Schütte-Lanz and 'the Super-Zeppelin of 1916'. The lower two show the frameworks of a Super-Zeppelin and a Schütte-Lanz. Ten 'Super-Zeppelins' (this was the British name for them) had been built in 1916, beginning with *LZ62*. Four were shot down before the end of the year.

Wigborough, Essex, where the twenty-two crew members, after trying to burn their ship, were taken prisoner. The remains of this year-old Zeppelin were a godsend to British airship designers, and a close examination was ordered, the results of which had a considerable influence on the design of British rigid airships. In the same raid *L32* (Captain: Werner Peterson) was brought down just before 1.00 a.m. by 2nd Lieutenant Frederick Sowrey, using incendiary bullets. The airship crashed in flames at Great Burstead, near Billericay, killing the twenty-seven men on board. Another Zeppelin in the same raid, *L31*, dropped its bombs on Streatham, Brixton, Kennington and Leyton, leaving twenty-two dead and seventy-five injured.

L31 was back a week later, with six other navy airships, heading for London. Bombs were dropped on Cheshunt before *L31* (Captain: Heinrich Mathy) was shot down by 2nd Lieutenant Wulstan Tempest, killing the sixteen crew members.

On 27/28 September 1916 ten Zeppelins flew towards the Midlands and the North. *L34* (Captain: Max Dietrich) was hit near Hartlepool by a BE2c and fell burning into the sea. All twenty men on board died. *L21* (Captain: Kurt Frankenberg) was shot down by two more BE2cs, killing all sixteen on board.

In 1916 twenty-two raids (including those on London, Edinburgh, Leith and Sunderland) killed nearly 300 and injured 480. But the British defences had improved and there were now better aeroplanes, new incendiary bullets, more effective searchlights and guns. By the end of 1916 over a hundred aeroplanes were employed in defending the country against air attack, as well as more than 17,000 men of the RFC.

1917

The German Army and Navy responded differently to the increasing losses of airships: the army disbanded its airship service in the summer of 1917; the navy decided that the answer was to fly so high that they could not be reached by British aeroplanes, and in February 1917 the first 'height-climber', *L42*, came into service. It was similar to earlier Zeppelins, but made lighter by removing as much as possible to save weight, including one engine. *L44* was completed at Löwenthal in April 1917 – it had a lighter frame, and a streamlined gondola.

The Germans were making increasing use of aeroplanes and on 25 May 1917 twenty-one Gothas bombed Folkestone and Shorncliffe, killing ninety-five and injuring 195. In June there were raids on Shoeburyness and Sheerness, and then twenty-two Gothas arrived over London, killing thirteen at Liverpool Street Station, and eighteen children at Upper North Street School in Poplar. That day's totals were 162 dead, 432 injured.

Four days after this London raid the Zeppelin *L42*, shot down by three British aeroplanes, came to earth near Thebberton in Suffolk; only two of the crew survived.

During the year 1917 there were seven raids by airships. They killed forty and injured seventy-five. In the same year there were twenty-eight raids by aeroplanes, which killed 655 and injured 1,532.

1918

In early January 1918 German airship operations received a huge blow when four Zeppelins and a Schütte-Lanz (*L46, L47, L51, L58* and *SL20*) were destroyed by fire in their sheds at Ahlhorn. On 19 July 1918 the British launched the first successful attack by carrier-borne aeroplanes when *L54* and *L60* were destroyed at Tondern by Sopwith Camels from HMS *Furious*.

46 Launched in 1917, the Schütte-Lanz *SL20* was 650ft long x 75ft maximum diameter, and powered by five 240hp Maybach engines. The *SL20* was destroyed in a hangar fire at Ahlhorn in January 1918.

In August *L70* (Captain: Johannes van der Haegen) – on its first raid – was hit by explosive ammunition fired by two DH4 aeroplanes; twenty-two men died when it broke in two and fell into the sea off the Norfolk coast. A week later *L53* (Captain: Edouard Prölss) was shot down near the Dutch coast by a Sopwith Camel, with the loss of twenty-two men. Airships attempted a total of four raids in 1918: sixteen people were killed by bombs and twenty injured. There were nine aeroplane raids, which killed 182 and injured 430.

THE AFRICA SHIP

The aim of the Africa Ship venture was to support the force commanded by Paul von Lettow-Vörbeck in East Africa. Strasser, the head of airship operations, was enthusiastic, writing in September 1917 that 'completion of the operation will not only provide immediate assistance for the brave Protectorate troops, but will be an event that will once more enthuse the German people and arouse admiration throughout the world.' It was decided that the mission should start from the German base at Jamboli in Bulgaria.

The new Zeppelin *L59* was assigned the task, making its first flight on 30 October 1917. It was 743ft long x 78ft diameter, with a capacity of 2,420,000 cubic feet, and there were five 240hp Maybach engines, driving the airship at a maximum speed of 64mph. *L59* left Staaken on 3 November, arriving at Jamboli twenty-eight hours later. The dirigible would not be able to return from East Africa, so it was planned that every part of the craft would be converted to another use: the framework would be a wireless mast, clothing and tents could be fashioned from the canvas, leather was for boots. Fifteen tons of cargo was stowed, including thirty machine-guns and 400,000 rounds of ammunition. Ludwig Buckholt and his crew of twenty-two left Jamboli on 13 November 1917, but bad weather forced them back, having jettisoned a ton of cargo.

They tried again a week later – on 21 November they passed over the coast of Egypt, on the night tof 22nd they were at Wadi Halfa. Buckholt now received a wireless message ordering him to turn back because of the military situation at their destination. Most of the cargo was thrown overboard, and *L59* left Africa behind on the night of 24/25 November. The crew – suffering from extreme cold and exhaustion – were thankful to reach Jamboli, having been in the air for ninety-five hours covering 4,340 miles. Ludwig Buckholt was awarded the highest German decoration, the *Pour le Mérite*.

By late October 1918 Germany was in turmoil. At Kiel, sailors of the High Seas Fleet had mutinied, and throughout Germany various groups tried to seize power; at Friedrichshafen, Zeppelin and Maybach workers demonstrated at the Town Hall in support of a German republic. On 5 November there was a general strike at Friedrichshafen, a soldiers' and workers' council was formed, and there were demands for the abdication of the Kaiser – which came on 9 November – and an end to the war. An Armistice came into effect on 11 November 1918.

During the First World War the German Army lost fifty per cent of its airships and the navy lost seventy per cent. Their raids on Britain killed 550 people and injured more than 1,400.

BRITISH AIRSHIPS IN THE FIRST WORLD WAR

The Naval Wing of the Royal Flying Corps became the Royal Naval Air Service by Admiralty regulations issued on 23 June 1914. It was to consist of: the Air Department of the Admiralty, a Central Office at Sheerness, and a Royal Naval Flying School at Eastchurch. Royal Naval Air Stations had to be constructed, and by the war's end they had been established at Anglesey, Capel (Kent), Cranwell (Lincolnshire), East Fortune (East Lothian), Howden (Yorkshire), Kingsnorth (Kent), Longside (Angus), Luce Bay (Wigtonshire), Mullion (Cornwall), Pembroke, Polegate (Sussex) and Pulham (Norfolk). There were, in addition, about fifteen mooring-out stations.

The Submarine Scout Class

The First World War began for Britain on 4 August 1914. At that time the RNAS possessed thirty-nine aeroplanes, fifty-two seaplanes and seven airships: *No.2* (Willows); *No.3* (Astra-Torres); *No.4* (Parseval), *Beta*, *Gamma*, *Delta* and *Eta*.

From 28 Augus*t No.3* spent a week moored-out at Ostend, patrolling the Belgian coast. *Beta II* spent a month at Dunkirk early in 1915.

Within six months it was to become obvious that many more airships would be needed. On 4 February 1915 the Germans announced that a blockade would be enforced in the seas around the British Isles and all merchant shipping would be liable to attack. The main weapon to enforce this blockade would be the submarine.

On 28 February the British First Sea Lord, Admiral Fisher, sent for Commander E.A.D Masterman, head of the navy's airship section. Fisher wanted more airships – quickly. Specifically, he wanted a U-boat hunter which could stay on patrol for about eight hours, be flown by two men, and be capable of carrying wireless equipment and 160lb of bombs. It should have a range of thirty to forty miles, with a top speed of 50mph. In view of the

47 An aeroplane fuselage fitted as a gondola to *SS23*. In the front is the wireless operator, in the centre the pilot, and at the rear is the observer. The trailing rope is for the ground crew.

urgent need, it must be a straightforward design, capable of being produced quickly and in quantity.

A prototype, constructed at Kingsnorth, was in the air within three weeks of Fisher's request: the envelope was taken from the navy's *No.2* (Willows) and the gondola was the fuselage of a BE2c aeroplane. The First Sea Lord immediately ordered a dozen more, to be known as the *Submarine Scout* type. The *SS1* took off on 7 May to visit the new airship station at Capel. Following a main road *SS1* hit some telegraph wires, fire broke out, and the envelope was completely destroyed, although the fliers escaped unhurt.

SS2, designed by Ernest Willows and built by Airships Ltd, was not accepted by the Admiralty; *SS3* (143ft long and driven by a Renault engine) appeared in April 1915 and altogether forty-nine were built.

Submarine Scout – Pusher (SSP)

A big problem with the *SS* type was that the crew had to operate from an open cockpit, exposed to the stream of air pulled back by the propeller. The *SSP* put the propeller aft, driven by a 75hp Rolls-Royce Hawk engine. The *SSP* type was 143ft long x 30ft, with a capacity of 70,000 cubic feet. A crew of four could be carried. The first airship of this type flew in January 1917 – six were built: three were lost in 1917 but the rest were still in service at the end of the war.

Submarine Scout Zero

By July 1917 sixteen *SS Zeros* were in service with the RNAS. Designed and built at Capel Airship Station, each airship had a boat-shaped gondola, with a cockpit opening for each of the three crew members: a pilot, an engineer and a wireless operator. In order to cut down the time taken to get to the sea areas to be patrolled 'mooring-out' sites were set up. These were often in or near small woods, with the airship fastened to a mast and RNAS

48 *SS Zero 65* making ready to land at RNAS Longside, Peterhead, in 1918.

personnel living in tents. Over seventy *SS Zeros* went into service, plus two for the French and two for the United States Navy.

Submarine Scout Twin

SSTs were bigger than the *Zeros*: 100,000 cubic feet, five crew members, and a 17ft-long gondola with an outrigger on each side to carry the two Rolls-Royce Hawk engines. Thirteen were delivered during the war, of which three were bought by the United States.

Coastal Class

The first of the *Coastal* class was delivered to the RNAS in January 1916. Flown by a crew of three, the airship used an Astra-Torres envelope, was 196ft long x 39ft maximum diameter, and could stay in the air for over twenty hours. Two machine-guns were installed on top of the envelope, reached by a rope ladder. The RNAS commissioned twenty-seven, which were based at Howden, Pulham, East Fortune, Longside and (for training) at Cranwell.

Four were bought by Russia and one by France. Of the twenty-seven in service with the RNAS twelve were lost.

C Star Class

Ten were produced, all entering service in 1918: 210,000 cubic feet, 218ft long x 47ft diameter, with two engines.

North Sea Class

Designed and built at Kingsnorth, the first five (of fourteen) came into service in 1917. They were 262ft long x 57ft diameter, with a capacity of 360,000 cubic feet. The airships

49 One of the twenty-seven *Coastal Class* airships deployed by the Royal Naval Air Service.

had an endurance of over twenty hours, and the crew (in two watches of five men each) had the luxury of an enclosed cabin. These dirigibles were all based at East Fortune, except for *NS14*, which was sold to the United States.

Semi-Rigid

The *Submarine Scout, Coastal, C Star* and *North Sea* classes were all of non-rigid construction. The Italian 'M' class airship which was bought by Britain in October 1918 was of semi-rigid construction. Designated *SR1*, it was 269ft long x 59ft diameter, 441,000 cubic feet, with a crew of nine. The engines were two 200hp Itala-Maybach and one 200hp SPA6a. The captain and pilot for the flight to Britain was George Meager, with eight other men on board. They left Ciampino, near Rome, in the early hours of 28 October 1918 and arrived at Kingsnorth on 31 October after a difficult and wearing journey. George Meager was awarded the Air Force Cross and the Italian Croce di Guerra. A month after arrival in Britain the airship was used to observe the surrender of German U-boats at Harwich, and in July 1919 it flew over London and south Wales, before being deleted in the September.

British Rigid Airships Completed During the War

The experience with *Mayfly* had cooled the navy's interest in rigid airships, but German progress in this field forced reconsideration. Even so, it was only late in the war that British rigids entered service, and they were to play little part in operations.

50 The first *North Sea* airship went into service in 1917. The crew of ten had the benefit of an enclosed gondola.

HMA No.9

The design of *No.9*, the first British rigid airship to fly, was strongly influenced by information gleaned from the Zeppelin *LZ16* which had landed at Lunéville in April 1913. The Admiralty awarded a contract to Vickers in March 1914, and a new shed and gasbag factory were erected at Walney Island. Progress was slow: the Vickers design team, dispersed after the *Mayfly* experience, had to be gathered together again; in January 1915 Walney was shelled by the German submarine *U-21*; in March 1915 the project was cancelled, but work began again later in the year.

No.9 was 526ft long x 53ft diameter, with a capacity of 866,000 cubic feet, and four 180hp Maybach engines (built by Wolseley, a Vickers subsidiary). The first flight was made on 27 November 1916, but the airship could not lift the weight specified in the contract and so was rejected by the Admiralty. To save weight the two engines were taken out and a 240hp Maybach engine substituted – it had been salvaged from the German Navy's *L33*, brought down in Essex two months before.

Accepted in April 1917, HMA *No.9* was sent to the Rigid Airship Trial Flight, which had been established at Howden a year earlier. By now obsolescent, the airship was scrapped a year later.

23 Class

Designed in 1915, these airships were modified versions of *No.9*: they were 942,000 cubic feet, 525ft long x 53ft diameter, with four 250hp Rolls-Royce engines, and a crew of seventeen. Three gondolas were slung underneath and there was a 45ft long cabin. A gun could be positioned on top of the envelope and four 100lb bombs were carried.

Orders were given to three manufacturers in October 1915: Vickers would build *No.23*, Beardmore *No.24* and Armstrong Whitworth *No.25*. In January 1916 *No.26* was ordered

51 *HMA No.9* was the first British rigid airship to fly – on 27 November 1916. It was accepted by the RNAS in April 1917 and sent to the Rigid Airship Trial Flight at Howden in Yorkshire.

from Vickers. Beardmore's and Armstrong's were provided with drawings and technical help by Vickers.

R23 was delivered to Pulham on 15 October 1917, to be employed on training and trials, including some with a 'parasite aircraft' – in 1918 a pilotless Sopwith Camel, with controls fixed, was attached to the underside of the airship and released in flight to glide to earth. Lieutenant Keys later piloted a Camel off the airship. *R23* was scrapped in September 1919.

R24 was built by William Beardmore & Company at Inchinnan, where a large construction shed was built with the aid of a government grant. *R24* was allocated to training and convoy protection, and after the Armistice came into effect it was used for mooring trials at the Pulham mast.

R25 was built by Armstrong Whitworth at Barlow, near Selby, where a shed was built with a government grant. The airship became a training craft at Cranwell, until deleted in September 1919.

R26 began its service at Howden in April 1918. Six weeks later it flew a continuous patrol of forty hours and forty minutes – the longest flight yet by a British rigid airship. In November 1918 it was at the surrender of the German U-boats at Harwich, and was scrapped four months later.

23 Class: This type of airship was 539ft long x 53ft diameter; capacity 990,000 cubic feet. The crew could move between gondolas by means of a corridor inside the envelope.

R27, built by Beardmore, was accepted in June 1918. On 16 August it was destroyed by fire in its shed at Howden, together with *SS Zeros 38* and *54*.

Construction of *R28* began at Beardmore's, moved to Vickers in the summer of 1917, and was cancelled in the autumn. *R29* (Armstrong Whitworth) was commissioned at East Fortune in June 1918, and deleted in October 1919. *R30* was cancelled before construction work began.

31 Class: In 1916 the Admiralty awarded Short Brothers a contract to build two wooden-framed rigid airships: *R31* and *R32*. The firm was lent the money to buy a site for construction at Cardington, Bedfordshire, where a shed was built: 700ft long, 180ft wide, and 110ft high.

R31 had a capacity of 1,547,000 cubic feet, was 615ft long x 65ft diameter, with six 300hp engines and a top speed of 70mph. Machine-gun posts were sited on top of the envelope. After test flights in July 1918 one engine was removed. In October a vertical fin crumpled. On 6 November 1918 (five days before the Armistice) *R31* started its flight from Cardington to East Fortune but on the way it had to make an unscheduled landing at Howden, where it was housed in the shed in which the three airships had burned less than three months earlier. The roof of the shed let in the rain, and *R31*'s wooden frame started to rot. The airship was dismantled in February 1919, having flown for a total of nine hours.

R32 spent a month with the Royal Navy in 1919 before being transferred to the Royal Air Force, when it was used for experiments by the National Physical Laboratory, and for training US Navy crews for the *R38*/ZR-2. It was deleted in 1921.

During the war dirigibles had been employed around the coasts of the British Isles: on reconnaissance and anti-submarine patrols, looking for mines, and escorting and protecting convoys. Some airships went further afield: in August 1915 an airship detachment (with three Submarine Scouts) went to the Dardanelles, establishing its headquarters first at Imbros and then at Mudros. Late in 1916 an airship was based at Dunkirk and another was lent to the RFC to support operations in France. In 1917 a detachment went to Italy to provide support for the airships which had been bought from Britain.

At the start of the First World War there had been 198 people in the Navy's Airship Section, and only three small airships were operational. At the end (November 1918) 5,800 people were serving, with more than a hundred airships.

FRANCE

The French Naval Air Service grew from eight aircraft and thirty-two pilots to (at the time of the Armistice) 1,264 aeroplanes, thirty-seven airships, and 700 pilots. In January 1916 there were three airship stations (with one shed at each) – Bizerta, Le Havre and Marquise; by November 1918 there were fourteen stations – in addition to the three mentioned they were at Ajaccio, Algiers, Aubagne, Corfu, Guipavas, Issy-les-Moulineaux, Montebourg, Oran, Paimboeuf, Rochefort and St Cyr.

The role of the French airships was to escort convoys and detect mines and submarines, but they had to operate in varied environments with a wide range of temperatures – the Channel, the Atlantic and the Mediterranean. By 1916 there were six airships in commission – three *SS Class* (60,000 cubic feet) bought from Great Britain; one Zodiac (70,000 cubic feet); one *Coastal* (170,000 cubic feet) bought from Britain, and the Chalais-Meudon *Tunisie* (370,000 cubic feet) which had been taken over from the army; it was driven by two 220hp Clément engines and was armed with two 47mm guns and 1,760lb of bombs.

Six more airships were transferred from the army to the navy in April 1917. Two British *SS Zeros* were bought in 1917 and, in addition, five of the Zodiac *Vedette* type came into service, followed by ten more in 1918. Late in 1918 another eight were commissioned, with a larger capacity and more powerful engines. The *VZ1–15* (90,000 cubic feet) had

52 The French Zodiac *d'Arlandes*. It was transferred from the army to the navy in April 1917.

53 The view from the gondola of a French airship, 1918.

two 80hp Renault engines with a top speed of 45mph. Their range at cruising speed was twelve hours. There was a crew of three, and a bomb load of 220lb. *VZ16 – 23* (110,000 cubic feet) were fitted with two 150hp Hispano engines.

Apart from these scouts, airships constructed during the war for the French Navy (all of them non-rigid) included: *Chalais Meudon 1–4* (190,000 cubic feet), *Chalais-Meudon 5–8* (320,000 cubic feet; crew of eight, 1,300 tons of bombs, one 75mm gun); *Astra-Torres AT1–4*

(230,000 cubic feet), *AT5–9* (260,000 cubic feet), *AT10–17* (300,000 cubic feet, crew of six, endurance thirty hours, one 75mm gun, 880lb of bombs); *Zodiac ZD1–5* (217,000 cubic feet), *ZD6–8* (330,000 cubic feet, one 75mm gun, 1,760lb of bombs).

Towards the end of the war a rigid airship was ordered with 2,000,000 cubic feet capacity, capable of staying airborne for three days, and proposals for eleven more rigids were at the design stage, but no French rigid airship was to appear.

ITALY

Italian airships had designations of P (Piccolo – small), M (Medium), V (Velore – fast) and G (Grande – large).

Italy entered the First World War on the side of the Allies on 23 May 1915, when it declared war on Austro-Hungary. At that time the Italian forces had a total of nine airships: with the army were *P5* (155,380 cubic feet) at Boscomantico, near Verona; *M1* (441,430 cubic feet) at Campalto, near Venice; *M3* and *M4*; and the Parseval *PL17* (not used in the war). The navy had *M2 Città di Ferrara* at Jesi, near Ancona; *V1 Città di Jesi* (517,350 cubic feet) at Ferrara and *P4* at Campalto. *V2* was being built. All, except the Parseval, were semi-rigid.

Most of these did not see out the war: in 1915 *M2* took off on a mission to bomb Fiume; it was shot down by an Austrian seaplane, but the crew members were rescued,

54 The Italian *M* type/British *SR1*, which was flown to Britain in 1918.

although two died. The wreckage of the airship was put on show in Pula. *V1* was shot down by anti-aircraft guns over Pula, and *P5* was taken out of service; on 4 May 1916 *M4* was brought down over the front line at Gorizia; *M3* was hit by anti-aircraft fire on 21 May 1917 near Casarsa and, later in the year, *V2* was decommissioned.

Italian airships made many raids during the war, attacking targets such as railway junctions, the naval base at Pula and shipbuilding yards at Trieste. They were also employed on mine spotting, and reconnaissance in the mountains of northern Italy. Alongside airships the use of aeroplanes developed rapidly in the war, and by early 1916 the Corpo Aeronautico Militare had seven squadrons of bombers.

Fifty airships – all semi-rigid – were commissioned during the war, the largest classes being the *M* and the *DE*. The sixteen *M* craft, constructed by the Military Aircraft Factory in Rome, were modified as the war went on: there were two, three or sometimes four engines on outriggers fitted to the sides of the gondola. The *M* types were 260ft long, had a capacity of 441,400 cubic feet, and could reach a height of 15,000ft. They were fitted with a ballonet running the whole length of the envelope, which was divided into six gas-holding compartments. A gun was installed on top of the envelope and a bomb load of over 2,000lb could be carried. Of the *M* types commissioned in the war: *M5* crashed at Mirafiori, Turin, after colliding with an aeroplane; the navy *M8* was destroyed by bombs in its shed at Ferrara and *M13* was shot down.

There were also sixteen of the *DE* class, built at the Military Aircraft Factory. Much smaller than the M type, their capacity varied from 60,000 cubic feet to 92,000 cubic feet.

A new Forlanini semi-rigid (529,700 cubic feet; 295ft long x 59ft diameter) appeared in each of the years 1915, 1917 and 1918. *F4* went to the navy and *F5* and *F6* to the army. *F5* burned in its shed at Baggio in March 1919.

The navy received *PV0*, *PV1*, *PV2* and *PV3* in 1918. They had a capacity of 183,600 cubic feet, and were 196ft long x 59ft diameter. In the same year the navy also took delivery of four of Nobile and Pesce's O type (127,000 cubic feet, 177ft long x 34ft) and four British *Submarine Scouts*.

UNITED STATES OF AMERICA

DN-1

The United States entered the First World War on 6 April 1917. Four months earlier the US Navy had taken delivery of its first airship, from the Connecticut Aircraft Company of New Haven. *DN-1* was 176ft long x 35ft diameter, with a capacity of 110,000 cubic feet, and two 140hp engines built by Sturtevant & Co. It was housed in a new floating shed at the Naval Air Station, Pensacola, Florida.

A test flight was planned for 20 April 1917, when it was found that the envelope was leaking, and that the airship was carrying too much weight. One engine was taken out, but *DN-1* made only two more ascents. (It was sometimes, retrospectively, referred to as the '*A Class*').

55 *DN-1* approaching the floating shed at Pensacola. This was the US Navy's first airship, delivered just before America's entry into the First World War.

56 A *B Class* blimp. Sixteen were ordered in March 1917. They were 160ft long x 32ft maximum diameter, and flown by a crew of three.

B Class

The non-rigid airships ('blimps') *B-1* to *B-16* were ordered in March 1917 from Goodyear (9), Connecticut Aircraft (2), Goodrich (2) and Curtiss (3). Those ordered from Curtiss were, in fact, built by Goodrich after it was decided that Curtiss would concentrate on producing the gondolas (using the fuselage of their *JN-4* aeroplane), fins and engines. Flown by a crew of three, B Class airships were 163ft long x 32ft diameter, 84.000 cubic feet capacity, and armed with a Lewis gun. They could cruise at 35mph, and stay on patrol for over twenty-four hours

   B-1 was built at the White City Amusement Park, Chicago; and first flew on 24 May 1917, piloted by Goodyear's chief engineer, Ralph H. Upson. *B-1* and *B-2* (which was also built in Chicago) were employed as training ships at Wingfoot Lake, where the Goodyear Company was contracted to train navy airship personnel.

   The rest of the B Class airships were assigned to protect shipping, operating from the Naval Air Stations at Cape May, Chatham, Hampton Roads, Key West. Montauk, Pensacola and Rockaway.

C Class

Ten non-rigid *C Class* airships were built by Goodyear and Goodrich, with gondolas by Curtiss. *C-1* made its first flight, at Wingfoot Lake, on 30 September 1918. Driven by two 150hp Hispano-Suiza engines, it was 196ft long x 42ft diameter; 181,000 cubic feet capacity. *C-1* could carry four 270lb bombs and was fitted with a Lewis gun. This blimp, while in flight, dropped off a Curtiss *JN-4* 'parasite' aeroplane.

   It was planned to use *C-5* with a crew of six, commanded by Lieutenant Commander E.W. Coil, for an attempt at crossing the Atlantic. On 14 May 1919 the airship flew from Montauk to Newfoundland (1,200 miles) non-stop in just under twenty-six hours, but, as the airship was being made ready for the Atlantic attempt, it was blown away – there was no one on board – to be found in a deflated state nearly seventy miles out to sea.

   The last of the *C Class* was delivered in March 1919; two were transferred to the army.

American Crews in Europe

American airmen did not fly their airships on operations from Britain, but some were trained at Cranwell, and some served on RNAS airships. In August 1917 Lieutenants Zachary Lansdowne and Ralph Kiely were sent to train in Britain, finishing at RNAS Cranwell in November. In the same month the first pilots who had trained at Wingfoot Lake arrived at the French base of Paimboeuf, on the estuary of the Loire. The US detachment, commanded by Lieutenant Commander Maxfield, trained on the French airships *AT-1* (*Astra-Torres*) and *VZ-3* (*Zodiac Vedette*). On 17 August 1917 the assistant secretary of the navy (F.D. Roosevelt) paid a visit to Paimboeuf, and was flown in *AT-1*.

   At the Armistice on 11 November 1918 American crews based at Paimboeuf were flying *AT-13*, *VZ-7* and *VZ-13*. Paimboeuf had become a US Naval Air Station on 1 March 1918, and another air station became operational on the day hostilities ended: Guipavas, near Brest, where the Americans flew *Capitaine Caussin*. The last official trip was made when *AT-13* and *Capitaine Caussin* flew to greet President Wilson on his arrival in Europe for the Peace Conference.

IV
BETWEEN THE WARS

After the end of the First World War Allied governments were determined to extract the maximum reparations from Germany. A month after the Armistice came into effect Sir Eric Geddes, in a speech at Cambridge, said that the Germans 'are going to be squeezed, as a lemon is squeezed – until the pips squeak'.

Article 198 of the Treaty of Versailles stated that 'The armed forces of Germany must not include any military or naval air forces', and *Article 202* specified the 'aeronautical material' which 'must be delivered to the Governments of the Principal Allied and Associated Powers' as reparations. As far as airships were concerned this included: 'Dirigibles able to take to the air, being manufactured, repaired or assembled … Plant for the manufacture of hydrogen … Dirigible sheds and shelters of every kind.' It was stipulated that:

> Pending their delivery, dirigibles will, at the expense of Germany, be maintained inflated with hydrogen; the plant for the manufacture of hydrogen, as well as the sheds for dirigibles may at the discretion of the said Powers, be left to Germany until the time when the dirigibles are handed over.

Commissions were set up to enforce the naval, military and air provisions – the latter becoming the province of the *Aeronautical Inter-Allied Commission of Control* (which was replaced in May 1922 by a small *Guarantee Committee*).

The German government was given an ultimatum in June 1919, seven months after the Armistice came into effect: sign the Treaty or face a renewal of the war. On 21 June the German Navy scuttled more than fifty of its warships in Scapa Flow, and two days later German crews destroyed seven naval airships at Nordholz (*L14, L41, L42, L63* and *L65*) and at Wittmund (*L52* and *L56*). The airships at Ahlhorn (*L64* and *L71*) were not touched. The Treaty of Versailles was signed on 28 June 1919, formally ending the First World War. As a result of the sabotage the Aeronautical Inter-Allied Commission demanded that all remaining airships be handed over. They were to be given to Belgium (naval airship *L30*), France (naval airship *L72*, army airship *LZ113* and the passenger craft *Nordstern*), Italy (*Bodensee* and the naval airship *L61*), Japan (naval airship *L37*) and the United Kingdom (naval airships *L64* and *L71*).

The Aeronautical Inter-Allied Commission also supervised the demolition of airship sheds, although Staaken was spared and used as a film studio, and Friedrichshafen survived because it had to build a new airship for the American government (to replace that destroyed by its crew on 23 June 1919).

FRANCE

The German reparations airship, the newly built naval rigid *L72*, a height-climber, was delivered to the French Navy at Maubeuge in July 1920, and given the name *Dixmude*.

Early in August it was moved to Cuers-Pierrefeu, near Toulon.

A year later, no flights had been made, but it was found that the gas cells needed to be replaced. A contract for this was given to the Astra-Nieuport company, but the new cells were not delivered until June 1923. Two months later the *Dixmude* was airborne for eighteen hours.

In the autumn of 1923 the airship undertook a programme of lengthy flights, the first lasting for fifty hours over North Africa, returning via Sardinia and Corsica. *Dixmude* left Cuers-Pierrefeu on Tuesday 25 September and returned to base on the evening of Sunday 30 September, a non-stop flight of more than 118 hours and over 4,350 miles. Under the command of Lieutenant de Vaisseau Jean du Plessis de Grenedan, the route followed was: Toulon–Marseilles–Balearic Islands–Algiers–Bizerta–cruise over Tunisia. The homeward journey across the Mediterranean began on Thursday afternoon, but a gale blew *Dixmude* back to Bizerta. On Friday: Sicily–Corsica–Marseilles–Bordeaux–Paris. The airship then departed for Trevol, where it circled the memorial to the *République* disaster of 25 September 1909.

From 17-19 October the *Dixmude* made a 'public relations' flight over France: Toulouse – Bordeaux–Rochefort–Nantes–Tours–Lyons. A month later it was exercising with the French fleet.

On 21 December 1923, having flown to southern Algeria, *Dixmude* exploded in mid-air off the coast of Sicily. All fifty men on board died, a tragedy which ended French interest in the development of airships.

Of the other reparations airships, *LZ113*, which had been taken by the army, never flew. The passenger Zeppelin *Nordstern* had been delivered to the army at St Cyr in June 1921, and renamed *Méditerranée*. For a year it was a training vehicle for the *Dixmude* crews, before being transferred to the navy in July 1922. It was then employed on local training and experimental flights until deleted in 1926.

GERMANY

The Zeppelin *Bodensee* (706,300 cubic feet, nearly 400ft long x 61ft diameter, with four 245hp Maybach engines) made its first flight on 20 August 1919. The gondola was divided into five compartments, each seating four people, and there was also a private cabin. There were sixteen crew members.

Four days after the first flight DELAG began a service between Berlin (Staaken) and Friedrichshafen. It was scheduled to operate from June to October, flying from Berlin to Friedrichshafen (in four hours) on even-numbered days, and the reverse trip on odd-numbered days. A few calls were made at Munich.

The *Bodensee* landed at Stockholm on 8 October 1919 to publicise the plans of Svenska Lufttrafik for a service between Berlin and Stockholm, but nothing came of this because of the handover of German airships to the Allies.

A month after the flight to Sweden *Bodensee* got into difficulties at Staake, arriving from Friedrichshafen with a full load of passengers, the engines failed. One of those on board was Mrs Tower, whose husband, Charles, was the Berlin correspondent of the *Daily Mail*: 'After repeated bumping the airship suddenly rose. There was a moment of extreme peril as we only just cleared the shed. We rose steadily to what seemed an immense height. We were in darkness, snow was falling, and it was terribly cold, as all the windows had been smashed.' It took about two hours to get the engines going, but there was so little fuel left that only one could be used, and it was not possible to return to Staaken. *Bodensee* came down near Cröchen, north of Magdeburg and nearly a hundred miles from Staaken:

> Between 3 and 4 in the morning, in complete darkness, we descended on the tops of fir trees which were densely covered with snow. These were fortunately dwarf trees; the ship cushioned on to them, and we landed safely. Every one offered a prayer of thanksgiving … In the early dawn, huddled in hay carts, we were removed through deep snow to a little village, where we got food and warmth.

In January 1920 the Aeronautical Inter-Allied Commission instructed DELAG to stop flights, in accordance with the Versailles Treaty. Since the previous August *Bodensee* had carried 2,250 passengers, well over three tons of cargo and four tons of mail. The airship was destined to go to Italy as *Esperia*.

Bodensee's sister ship was the *Nordstern* – North Star – which was intended for the proposed Stockholm service, but had to be delivered to France (becoming *Méditérranée*) after its test flights.

Zeppelin LZ126/United States ZR-3 (Los Angeles)

LZ126 was built for the United States and paid for by Germany as reparations. The Allies agreed to waive the restrictions on airship construction, provided that the new airship was not intended for military purposes. Work began in July 1922: *LZ126* was to be 66oft long x 9oft diameter and 2,472,000 cubic feet capacity. Internally there was a series of twenty frames of duralumin lattice work, braced by lateral girders and steel wires, and fourteen gas containers made of cotton and goldbeaters' skin.

A crew of twenty-eight was accommodated in six cabins and two mess rooms, while the officers had the use of two cabins and a mess room. The captain had his own cabin. A gangway ran from one end of the airship to the other, and underneath its widest part was the gondola, which was built into the framework.

On 25 September 1924 what the press described as 'the last German Zeppelin' began a long trial and demonstration, flying through the night over Sweden and Denmark then back across the Baltic to Stettin and Berlin 'where every roof was crowded'. Enthusiastic crowds, many brought by special train, greeted the airship at Staaken where the *LZ126* circled around the field, dropping mail bags 'tied up in the old Imperial black, white and red colours'. Hundreds of schoolchildren were gathered around the Victory Column on the Königsplatz while the Zeppelin cruised over the main streets for half an hour. The rest of this non-stop valedictory tour took in Potsdam, Dresden, Bayreuth, Nuremberg, Augsburg, Ulm, Stuttgart and Friedrichshafen. The whole flight lasted thirty-two hours.

There was a final two-and-a-half-hour trip over Lake Constance on 9 October and the following day the airship was inspected by members of the diplomatic corps. Three days later, when *LZ126* began its voyage to America, the *Berliner Tageblatt* brought out a special edition.

The airship left Friedrichshafen, under the command of Hugo Eckener, at 6.30 a.m. on 12 October 1924. No smoking was allowed on board, but there was a stock of chewing tobacco and gum. Seven sacks of mail were carried.

Two hours after take-off the airship was beyond Basel, and by 5.00 p.m. had passed over the estuary of the Gironde, leaving France behind. The Zeppelin was using a new navigation aid: tuning into a radio transmission – it received a low note if it was on course and a higher-pitched one if it was not.

57 The *Graf Zeppelin* preparing for departure.

At 7.45 a.m. on 15 October 1924 the *LZ126* passed over the Statue of Liberty at 500ft, greeted by the whistles and foghorns of vessels in the harbour, before circling over New York City for forty minutes. The landing at Lakehurst, New Jersey, came at 9.55 a.m. after a journey of 5,000 miles in eighty hours and forty-five minutes.

In Friedrichshafen a torchlight procession of Zeppelin workers, led by the town band, went to the houses of Karl Arnstein and Ludwig Dürr, who both came out to speak to the crowd. A wreath was laid at Count Zeppelin's statue.

Graf Zeppelin (LZ127)

As things turned out, *LZ126* was not the last Zeppelin. In 1926 the restrictions on German airship construction were lifted and, with finance from the government and public sub-scription, work was started on *LZ127*. Designed by Ludwig Dürr, this was the largest airship in the world until the arrival of the British *R100*, three years later. There were five gondo-las, each with a Maybach engine, which could operate on either petrol or blau gas (a fuel similar to propane, invented by Hermann Blau). The airship's total capacity was 3,708,000 cubic feet (984,250 cubic feet of this was made up of separate cells of blau gas). It was 776ft long x 100ft maximum diameter.

At the front of the gondola was a steering cabin and immediately behind this was the navigation cabin. Behind this again were the wireless cabin and the kitchen. The largest room was the passengers' saloon, which boasted 'mahogany furniture, wine-coloured car-pets and curtains, and four large windows, giving an extensive view.' Within the structure of the airship were storage spaces for luggage and cargo, as well as the crew accommodation.

The new craft was named by Count Zeppelin's daughter on 8 July 1928 – the Count's birthday.

The *Graf Zeppelin* completed several long trial flights in September 1928 and, in early October became the first German airship to be seen over England since the wartime raids.

Unterer Laufgang über der Führer- u. Fahrgastgondel

58 Walkway inside the framework of the *Graf Zeppelin*.

The Zeppelin had left Friedrichshafen in the early morning of 2 October, intending to visit Berlin, and other parts of Germany which had given generously to the 'Eckener Fund' to build the airship. There were seventy people on board, the sleeping cabins were in use and meals were being served, as a dress-rehearsal for long-distance flights. Not long after passing Bamberg it was decided that the weather prevented an immediate visit to Berlin, so *Graf Zeppelin* turned west to Frankfurt and Rotterdam, appearing over Lowestoft and Yarmouth at about 9.00 p.m.

From over the North Sea, Lady Drummond Hay sent her report for the Hearst newspapers: 'It is a strange sensation, sleeping in cabins attached to gas bags swinging 7,000ft in the air between the full moon and the glassy North Sea.' There was no heating, only:

> …merciless cold driving through the canvas walls of this flying tent … I have visualised myself gracefully draped over a saloon window ledge romantically viewing the moonlit sky. The men have reminded each other not to forget evening jackets and boiled shirts in their baggage. We have drawn ourselves lovely pictures of dining elegantly in mid-air with Commodore Eckener at the head of a flower-decked table, but leather coats, woollies and furs will be our evening dress. Hot soup and steaming stew more welcome than cold caviar and chicken salad.

Returning via Bremen and Hamburg, the airship was over Berlin just before 9.00 a.m. It was President Hindenburg's birthday, and so a bouquet of flowers was dropped at the President's palace, where it was picked up and delivered by a policeman. By 5.30 p.m. the *Graf Zeppelin* was back safely at Friedrichshafen after a flight of thirty-four and a half hours. Dr Hugo Eckener announced that the airship had passed its final test.

59 The saloon of the *Graf Zeppelin*.

60 The control cabin of the *Graf Zeppelin*.

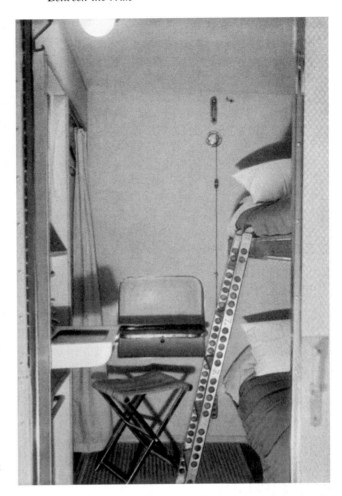

61 A sleeping cabin on
the *Hindenburg*.

The Zeppelin was considered to be ready to make the voyage to Lakehurst, New Jersey. This was to be the first ever transatlantic passenger flight – there were twenty passengers, including six press representatives (again with Lady Drummond Hay for the Hearst papers), five government officials, Count Alexander Brandenstein-Zeppelin (Count Ferdinand Zeppelin's son-in-law), Lieutenant Commander Charles E. Rosendahl (United States Navy) and Colonel Emilio Herrera (director of the Colon Transaerea Española, the company founded in September 1922 to run an air service between Seville and Buenos Aires).

The *Graf Zeppelin* left Friedrichshafen in the early morning of 11 October 1928 and arrived at Lakehurst at 5.30 p.m. local time, on 15 October after a flight of 112 hours.

The airship had arrived in America six miles north of Cape Charles, Virginia, and then made for Washington, passing over the White House. 'Crowds in the streets and on the housetops cheered and every whistle for miles around blew its loudest.' Next to be visited were Baltimore, Philadelphia and New York, before making for the landing place at Lakehurst. Reporters hoping for interviews with the passengers were disappointed, as they had all signed an undertaking not to say anything about the voyage for eight days. This restriction did not apply to Dr Eckener, who gave an account of how the bottom port fin had been damaged in a gale, which tore off part of the fabric leaving a hole about 50ft x 25ft. Four volunteers, including Hugo Eckener's son, had climbed over the duralumin framework in the dark, closing the hole with blankets and sheets taken from passengers' beds.

The return journey began at 2.00 a.m. on 29 October 1928, with sixty-four passengers and crew. Three US Naval officers were on board as observers: Commander M.R. Pierce (executive officer of the Naval Air Station, Lakehurst), Lieutenants G.W. Settle and C.E. Bauch (both of the *Los Angeles*). At 7.15 a.m. on 1 November the *Graf Zeppelin* landed at Friedrichshafen, to be welcomed by a large crowd, having covered 4,850 miles in just over seventy-one hours. The officers and crew were given a banquet that evening, and Dr Eckener received a telegram from President Hindenburg:

> Heartiest greetings on your safe return to the home port. The whole nation rejoices with me over the successful voyage of the storm-tried *Graf Zeppelin*, and is united in grateful and admiring acknowledgement of the magnificent work done by constructors, officers and crew. I hope soon personally to welcome you to Berlin.

From 25-29 March 1929 the *Graf Zeppelin* cruised in the Middle East with twenty passengers, including the President of the Reichstag Paul Loebe. The route took them over Marseilles, Corsica, Rome, Naples, Capri, Crete, Cyprus, Jaffa, Jerusalem, the Egyptian coast, Athens, Vienna (on the fourth night) and Friedrichshafen – a voyage of 5,000 miles, done in eighty-one hours.

Later in the year the *Graf Zeppelin* was to make the first passenger-carrying flight around the world, partially funded by William Randolph Hearst on condition that the circumnavigation should begin from Lakehurst. Much of the rest of the money came from the special envelopes franked for philatelists.

Lakehurst was left behind on 8 August 1929 – on board were thirty-seven crew members and sixteen passengers, including, once more, Hearst's reporter Lady Drummond Hay, and Sir Hubert Wilkins, the Arctic explorer who had been knighted the year before after flying from Alaska to Spitzbergen. Two days later the airship descended at Friedrichshafen, where the passengers went sightseeing.

The next leg of the voyage was non-stop over Siberia to Tokyo, where the *Graf Zeppelin* was housed in a shed transported from Germany. The 6,800 miles were covered in 101 hours. Then came the crossing of the Pacific: 5,800 miles in seventy-nine hours. Next, an overnight stay in Los Angeles, before the first non-stop airship flight across America: Kansas City, Chicago, Detroit, Cleveland and New York; covering 2,900 miles in fifty hours.

Lakehurst was reached on 29 August, twenty-one days, five hours and thirty-one minutes since setting out. The actual flying time was eleven days, twenty hours and thirty-four minutes. The next day Hugo Eckener and the crew were accorded a ticker-tape parade, which was described by *The Times* correspondent:

> Half a million people cheered and waved to them as they rode along Broadway behind companies of soldiers, bluejackets and police, who were wearing for the first time their smart new uniforms. Spools of ticker tape were unwound and the tape festooned itself over flagstaffs, the cornices of buildings, and on the motor cars in which the city's guests rode, flanked by a mounted police escort.

The navy airship *Los Angeles* floated above.

Thousands gathered at Friedrichshafen to watch the return home on 4 September 1929. The official reception party included the minister of communications, the Japanese ambassador, the United States ambassador and Count Zeppelin's daughter. In Berlin, flags were flown on all public buildings and school children were given a holiday.

1930 was a busy year for the *Graf Zeppelin*. On 16 April the airship was at Seville with, as usual, people crowding the streets and watching from rooftops, then Cadiz, then back to Seville. Ten days later the Zeppelin flew to England via Basel, Paris and Brighton; she cruised for some time over London, looming over Wembley Stadium during the Football Association Cup Final between Arsenal and Huddersfield Town. Seven passengers and three crew members were landed at Cardington and passengers boarded for the return journey, including: Air Vice-Marshal Sir Sefton Brancker, Air Commodore, and Mrs J.G. Weir, the Master of Sempill and Mrs Forbes-Sempill, Lieutenant Colonel V.C. Richmond, Commander H. Campbell (equerry to the Duke of York), Squadron Leader F.M. Rope, David Boyle, Miss Carstairs, Miss Jenkins, Mr Campbell-Begg, Dr and Frau Solmeson and Mr M.H. Vol. The Zeppelin again passed over London on the return journey to Friedrichshafen.

Graf Zeppelin, with its crew of forty and twenty passengers, left Friedrichshafen again on 8 May 1930, on a voyage planned to take three weeks: first to Seville (1,250 miles) and then to Pernambuco (3,750 miles). The next stage was Pernambuco to Rio de Janeiro and back to Pernambuco (2,500 miles), followed by Pernambuco–Havana–Lakehurst (5,000 miles), and finally from Lakehurst to Friedrichshafen, arriving home on 8 June. In New York Hugo Eckener talked of proposals for a regular transatlantic passenger and mail service, which it was planned to begin in just over a year's time, and he discussed the project with members of the International Zeppelin Transport Corporation, which had been formed in the previous year.

The *Graf Zeppelin* was in British skies again in July, during a cruise which took in the Faroe Islands, Orkney, Aberdeen, Edinburgh and Hull, before turning for Holland, Germany and Friedrichshafen.

Also in July, the Zeppelin joined in the celebrations at Mainz. The Rhineland had been occupied by the Allies, under the terms of the Versailles Treaty, for almost twelve years. On 30 June 1930 the Inter-Allied High Commission for the Rhineland left Wiesbaden, and the last French troops departed from Mainz. In Berlin thanksgiving services were held and all the church bells rang, a twenty-one-gun salute was fired, and flags flew from buildings, buses and tramcars. On 20 July President Hindenburg made a triumphal tour through the Rhineland, beginning at Speyer and then on through the wine-producing villages. At Mainz, the *Graf Zeppelin* flew over the Elector's Palace, to be greeted by cheering crowds and saluted from a balcony by the President.

Moscow was visited in September 1930, and after a stay of a few hours the airship made the return journey to Friedrichshafen in nineteen hours.

A second Middle Eastern cruise was undertaken from 9-13 April 1931; among the passengers were Group Captain Gossage (British air attaché, Berlin) and Squadron Leader Booth (of the British *R100*). The airship reached Alexandria, then flew up the Nile to Cairo, arriving thirty-three hours after leaving Friedrichshafen. The next task was to hover over the Great Pyramid, before cruising further up the valley of the Nile and landing at Cairo. Next day a trip was made to Jerusalem, Jaffa and Tel Aviv.

The Times of 17 June 1931 published the following letter to the editor: 'On board *Graf Zeppelin*, June 14 – To the redaction of *The Times*. Sir, for the first time in the world I have extraordinary permission to give an artistic representation in the airship *Graf Zeppelin*. With best regards from elevation of 2,000 metres, Yours, DÜCKER, Musical Clown.'

This in-flight entertainment by Dudu Dücker was described by a fellow-passenger:

> The door of the saloon opened and in tripped a clown in such a comic suit that we all burst into roars of laughter. Then this artist undressed, which took a very long time on account of his 25 waistcoats. In between he played all sorts of musical instruments in a masterly manner

and, accompanying himself, surprised us at the end with a wonderfully well-trained baritone voice which turned suddenly into soprano. The performance lasted perhaps half an hour. It seemed far too short for us.

Herr Dücker presented each passenger with a small mouth organ as a souvenir. At the end of the flight Dr Eckener gave the artist a hand-written testimonial: 'I thank you warmly for your successful performance in the airship *Graf Zeppelin* during the flight from Hannover to Friedrichshafen, the first of its kind in the history of Zeppelin airship transport' (*The Times*, 18 June 1931).

The *Graf Zeppelin* left Friedrichshafen on its Arctic exploration flight on 24 July 1931, after its load had been reduced as much as possible, with heavy furniture and crockery replaced by lightweight metal chairs and papier-mâché plates and cups. Emergency supplies for two months were loaded, as well as folding boats, sledges and skis.

The airship flew to the Arctic via Leningrad, and maintained wireless contact with the Soviet icebreaker *Malygin*, which it met off Hooker Island, east of Franz Josef Land. The Zeppelin hovered at about 250ft and dropped 'water anchors', each of which opened, like an umbrella, under the surface of the sea. The airship was then hauled down and settled on large air bags. Airship and icebreaker each launched a boat, and mails were exchanged (twenty-five per cent of the whole venture was financed with payments made by philatelists). Franz Josef Land was reached at around midnight, and the next day was spent making an aerial survey. The *Graf Zeppelin* arrived back at Friedrichshafen on 31 July, one week after it had set out.

Just over three months later, at 7.00 a.m. on 18 August 1931, a crowd of 50,000 saw the *Graf Zeppelin* land at Hanworth Air Park, Middlesex, after circling over central London. Hugo Eckener and the crew were welcomed by the under-secretary for air, who presented a gold box inscribed: 'Presented to Dr Hugo Eckener, on the occasion of his visit to the London Air Park with the *Graf Zeppelin* by some of his friends and admirers interested in the development of airships. "The winds and the wave are always on the side of the ablest navigators".'

The airship left for a cruise around Britain with passengers including Colonel the Master of Sempill, Lady Drogheda, Lieutenant Colonel F.C. Shelmerdine (director of civil aviation), Lord Newborough, Lord Inverclyde and Geoffrey Harmsworth. The route taken was: on Tuesday evening – Brighton, Worthing, Bognor, Ryde, and Bournemouth; (and on Wednesday) the coast of Ireland, Mull of Galloway, Carlisle, Tyneside, Leeds, Hull (at around midday), Great Yarmouth, London and Hanworth – landing at 7.15 p.m. After only twenty minutes on the ground the *Graf Zeppelin* left for Germany.

Following trial flights in 1931 a service to South America started in 1932, when nine return flights were made. In 1933 there were another nine – on the last one of the year Eckener flew the ship to Miami and then to Akron. On 26 October the *Graf Zeppelin* flew over the Century of Progress Exposition at Chicago, departing next day for Seville and Friedrichshafen.

By 1934 there were twelve round-trips a year to South America, by 1935 there were sixteen. Up to the end of that year the flights went as far as Pernambuco (either direct from Friedrichshafen or via Seville), but now new facilities were provided by the Brazilian government at Santa Cruz, near Rio de Janeiro. Another change which occurred in 1935 was that, two years after Adolf Hitler became chancellor, the German Air Ministry took over the Zeppelin manufacturing company and abolished DELAG, replacing it with DZR (Deutsche Zeppelin Reederei).

In 1937 the *Graf Zeppelin* was employed on twelve return flights to South America, while seven were undertaken by the *Hindenburg*.

LZ129/Hindenburg

The *Hindenburg* was built, with the aid of government funds, for the Atlantic crossing, which it could do in half the time taken by an ocean liner. It was designed to use helium, rather than the more flammable hydrogen, but the US Helium Control Act made this impossible.

Hindenburg was the largest airship yet built, being 7,500,000 cubic feet, 800ft long, with sixty crew and fifty passengers (increased to seventy-two in 1937). The passenger accommodation was contained within the hull: on the upper deck were cabins, a dining room, and a lounge complete with lightweight Blüthner piano; the lower deck had washrooms, rooms for the crew, and a smoking room – no matches were allowed but a steward controlled an electric lighter.

On 4 March 1936 the first flight was made, over Lake Constance, and two days later a seven and a half hour trip over the lake and then to Munich and Augsburg. The first long voyage came later in the month, to Rio de Janeiro. While Dr Eckener was on this flight *The Times* carried a report that the German Propaganda Ministry had forbidden the press to mention his name. The newspaper commented: 'It is difficult to believe that, whatever their political grievances against Dr Eckener, the Government would be willing to dispense with the professional genius and experience responsible for the post-War German triumphs in airship construction'. The ban was lifted a fortnight later.

The *Hindenburg*'s first journey to the United States began at 9.30 p.m. on 6 May 1936, arriving at Lakehurst on the 9th. On the second evening of the flight a half-hour broadcast was made to New York, including interviews with passengers and piano-playing by Franz Wagner of Dresden. Next morning Mass was celebrated by Father Schulte. The airship arrived over New York City after a flight of sixty hours and fifteen minutes, to be illuminated by a searchlight from the German liner *Bremen*, while ships and cars sounded their sirens and horns.

62 The dining room of the *Hindenburg*.

The *Hindenburg's* return journey began three days later. There was now a new terminus in Germany for the North and South American services: the *Rhine-Main Aerodrome and Zeppelin Port* at Frankfurt. The airship hangar was over 300 yards long, 170ft high and 170ft wide. The mooring-mast was on rails so that, with airship attached, it could be drawn right into the hangar. Hydrogen came from the German Dye Trust works at Höchst by means of an eight-mile pipeline.

Hindenburg's next North Atlantic flight, from Frankfurt, began on 17 May with the return from Lakehurst on the 20th. En route, the airship passed low over Keighley in Yorkshire at about 8.00 P.M. and a package was dropped over the town centre. Two boys, Alfred Butler and Jack Gerrard, found that it contained a spray of carnations and a note:

> Luftschiff *Hindenburg*. 22 May 1936. To the finder of this letter, please deposit these flowers and the Cross on the grave of my dear brother, Lieut. Franz Schulte, I Guards Foot Regiment. Prisoner of War in Skipton. Cemetery in Keighley, near Leeds. Many thanks for your kindness. Paul Schulte. The first flying priest. Please accept the stamps and the pictures as a small souvenir from me. God bless you! I said the first Holy Mass on the *Hindenburg*, 9 May 1936.

The boys were taken to Morton Cemetery, Keighley, where they laid the flowers at the foot of the memorial to German servicemen who had died while in captivity.

In 1936 the *Hindenburg* flew over 190,000 miles with 2,800 passengers, making seven voyages to Brazil and ten to the USA. On 1 August it was present at the opening ceremony of the Berlin Olympic Games.

63 The destruction of the *Hindenburg*.

The *Hindenburg* was destroyed by fire on 6 May 1937 while in the process of mooring at the Lakehurst mast. Mooring lines were dropped at 7.25 p.m., fire broke out, and the airship was quickly consumed by flames. Thirteen of the thirty-six passengers died and twenty-two of the sixty-one crew. The cause of the disaster was not established, but suggestions included sabotage, static electricity, lightning, sparks from an engine, inflammable paint, structural failure and a fuel leak. The German government cancelled all Zeppelin services.

The captain of the *Hindenburg*, Ernst August Lehmann, aged fifty-one, died of his injuries the day after the disaster. His career had been bound up with Zeppelin flight. An engineer, he was working in the naval dockyard at Kiel in 1913 when Hugo Eckener invited him to join DELAG, and Lehmann took command of the new *Sachsen*. In the First World War he commanded several airships before being made chief inspector of construction at Friedrichshafen, later becoming a director of the company. He flew to the United States in the *ZR-3/Los Angeles*, as second-in-command to Hugo Eckener, and stayed on for three years to develop the Goodyear-Zeppelin Company at Akron. Returning to Germany in 1928 he supervised the building of the *Graf Zeppelin*, taking part in the more important of the airship's voyages. The first flight of the *Hindenburg* to Lakehurst had been under his command.

LZ130/Graf Zeppelin

The new *LZ130* – another *Graf Zeppelin* – was 800ft long, capacity 7,100,000 cubic feet; powered by four 985hp Daimler-Benz engines, it could reach 80mph. In March 1938 Germany annexed Austria. Six months later the new *Graf Zeppelin* flew for the first time: Friedrichshafen, Munich, Augsburg, Ulm, Friedrichshafen. The airship was to make about thirty flights in all, including propaganda tours over Vienna and the Sudetenland. It also flew along the east coast of Britain, trying to collect information about radar installations.

The airship's final flight was on 20 August 1939, just before the start of the Second World War. In April 1940 the order came to scrap both of the *Graf Zeppelins* and the framework of the unfinished *LZ131*. Their metal was needed to build aeroplanes.

ITALY

The DELAG Zeppelin *Bodensee*, renamed *Esperia*, arrived in July 1921 as part of the reparations payments from Germany. Based at Ciampino, it was flown as a military airship, although there were some passenger flights, before it was scrapped in 1928.

From 1919 to 1931 eighteen airships, all of the semi-rigid type, were constructed in Italy. Of these, nine were exported: one to the Argentinian Navy, one to Japan, four to the Spanish Navy, two to the US Army and one to the US Navy.

Six of the Italian-built airships were of around 127,000 cubic feet; three of the others ranged from 180,000 to 250,000 cubic feet. The largest were the *Norge* and the *Italia* (both 653,300 cubic feet) and *Roma* (1,200,000 cubic feet) which was bought by the United States in November 1921.

The most famous personality in the Italian airship world was Umberto Nobile (1885–1978). Born near Naples, he was an engineer who, after five years of working for railways, turned to aeronautics. When Italy entered the war in 1915, Nobile was assigned to the Military Aircraft Factory and became involved in dirigible construction, having been given the rank of lieutenant-colonel.

64 The Zeppelin *Bodensee* was handed to Italy under the terms of the Treaty of Versailles. It arrived in July 1921, when it was renamed *Esperia*.

65 The gondola of the Italian *M1* airship converted to civilian use after the First World War. The double-deck cabin could seat thirty people.

Norge

Roald Amundsen, first to reach the South Pole, had made two attempts to fly over the North Pole in an aeroplane. He decided that his next try would be in a dirigible, choosing Nobile's semi-rigid *NR-1* for the task. This airship, which first flew in 1924, was 348ft long x 64ft diameter; 653,300 cubic feet, with three 250hp Maybach engines.

The expedition was financed by the American Lincoln Ellsworth, with the support of the Aero Club of Norway, which undertook to provide an airship shelter at King's Bay, Spitzbergen, 600 miles from the Pole. Nobile was engaged as pilot, and on 29 March 1926 at Ciampino, Amundsen formally took possession of the airship, which was renamed *Norge*.

On the way to Spitzbergen the airship visited Pulham in Norfolk, arriving on 11 April. A handling party of 300 men – volunteers from the surrounding countryside – had been ready from 10.00 a.m., but the airship did not arrive until 3.20 p.m. and was not housed until three hours later. The voyagers on the *Norge* (including Major Scott) were welcomed by an official party including the secretary of state for air and the crown prince of Norway. Air Vice-Marshal Sir John Salmond and his staff officers flew in from Manston in two Vickers Virginia bombers. A group from the Royal Airship Works turned up: Group Captain Fellowes, Lieutenant-Colonel Richmond, Squadron Leader Colmore and Flight Lieutenant Nixon.

At Pulham Nobile, speaking about the transpolar flight, told the press that 'If we have enough fuel we shall try to reach Nome in Alaska, as it will then be an easy matter to ship the various parts down to a suitable base in America.' But first the airship had to get

66 On 26 March 1926 Roald Amundsen took possession of the *Norge* at Ciampino, near Rome. Piloted by Umberto Nobile, the airship was the first to fly over the North Pole.

to Spitzbergen: *Norge*, with its crew of nineteen, left Pulham for Oslo at 11.45 p.m. on 13 April, carrying enough supplies for five days.

The *Norge* finally set off for the Pole, from Spitzbergen, on 11 May 1926, with sixteen men on board. They flew over the Pole, where they dropped American, Italian and Norwegian flags, and then carried on for another 1,000 miles, landing near Teller in Alaska. The flight, the first across the Arctic, had taken them seventy hours. Nobile was taken to meet the President of the United States, and Mussolini made him a general. *Norge* was dismantled and never flew again.

Italia

The *Italia*, almost identical with *Norge,* was used by Umberto Nobile on his own expedition to fly over the North Pole, with financial backing from the city of Milan and the Royal Geographical Society of Italy. With twenty men on board the *Italia* left Milan on 15 April 1928, arriving at Spitzbergen on 4 May. A week later an eight-hour trial flight was made, followed on 15 May by a long flight over Russia.

The North Pole attempt began on the 23rd, with *Italia* reaching the objective at about 12.30 p.m. after a twenty-hour flight; Italian and Milanese flags were dropped. Two hours later the return journey began, but mechanical problems developed, the weather deteriorated, ice built up, and the airship lost height rapidly. At about 10.00 a.m. on 25 May it crashed – the control gondola and engine compartment were torn off, while the rest of the airship disappeared into the air with six men, never to be seen again. Nine survivors and one dead man were left on the ice, with a few supplies, a radio, and Nobile's dog. Four of the survivors were injured, including Nobile whose right arm and leg were broken. Twelve days after the crash a Russian radio amateur picked up a distress signal and a rescue operation was mounted by several countries. Amundsen set off in a French aeroplane, but never returned.

Weeks later the survivors were located, and Nobile was taken off by a Swedish seaplane, leaving eight crew members behind; three weeks after this all were rescued by the Russian icebreaker *Krassin*. They had survived for forty-nine days.

SOVIET UNION

Umberto Nobile, having made himself unpopular with Mussolini's government, decided to accept an invitation to oversee the construction of airships in the Soviet Union.

In the 1920s two experimental craft had been built in Russia, the largest with a capacity of 84,755 cubic feet. Four non-rigids had been produced during the first Five Year Plan of 1928–1932, and on 7 November 1932, to celebrate the fifteenth anniversary of the revolution, they flew over Red Square in Moscow: *V1 USSR Patriot*, *V2 Smolny*, *V3 Red Star* and *V4 Komsomol Pravda*.

Airships were seen as having an important part to play in the development of the remote regions of the Soviet Union – they could be used for exploration and mapping, as well as the carriage of freight and passengers. Only primitive ground facilities existed, so the smaller non-rigids or semi-rigids were preferred as they could be moored in the open air and, if necessary, deflated quickly.

Umberto Nobile arrived in the USSR just as the Second Five Year Plan, 1933–1937, was being promulgated. It specified the construction of fifty semi-rigid airships of up to

3,500,000 cubic feet, four rigids of 4,400, 000 cubic feet and four of 8,500,000 cubic feet. To Nobile this was unrealistic, and he agreed to build three – an experimental semi-rigid of 70,500 cubic feet, a larger semi-rigid of 670,000 cubic feet, and a rigid of 3,500,000 cubic feet. Also in the plan was a small (35,300 cubic feet) all-metal craft designed by Konstantin Chiolovski. This had no internal framework and was built of 1mm-thick sheets of steel, with two internal girders to support the gondola. Nothing came of this project.

In spite of initial difficulties Nobile was to supervise the construction of five semi-rigid airships. *V6* (653,300 cubic feet, 320ft long) was similar to Nobile's 'N' Class and made its maiden flight over Moscow on 5 November 1934. Named *Osoviakhim* (after the Soviet organisation for promoting aviation, which had raised twenty million roubles to build the airship), it was intended for the route from Moscow to Sverdlovsk, but there were no facilities for refuelling or mooring until a mast was erected at Sverdlovsk in 1936. The *Osoviakhim* broke the world endurance record in October 1937, staying in the air for over 130 hours, beating the record set by the *Graf Zeppelin*. Five months later it was decided that the airship should make an attempt to rescue Soviet scientists who were trapped on disintegrating pack ice. On its way to Murmansk, on 5 February 1938, the airship crashed into a mountain, killing thirteen of the nineteen men on board.

V7 was destroyed by fire in its hangar in August 1934. It was replaced by *V7 bis* – *Chelyuskinets* – in the spring of 1935, but was lost when it crashed in the following October. Nobile's other airship, *V8*, was completed by the Soviet engineers, and operated from 1936 to 1938.

UNITED KINGDOM

At the Armistice of November 1918 Britain had about a hundred non-rigid military airships in commission. By January 1919 *The Times* was writing, under the heading 'Blimps for Pleasure':

> The airship, we are officially informed, will make an ideal pleasure craft, and there is no more pleasant means of viewing the beauties of the country than flying in the comfortable car of an airship a few hundred feet above the treetops. The small airship such as the Twin is less expensive than a steam yacht.

Blimps were still employed on military duties six months later, when *NS11* was lost. The crew of seven had left Pulham at midnight for a mine-sweeping patrol over the North Sea, but during a heavy storm the airship caught fire and fell into the sea, killing all on board.

With the war at an end, responsibility for the blimps passed to the Disposals Board, and in the summer of 1921 it was reported that: 'They have been sold for a mere song to anyone who would buy them, and the use to which they have been put is to become covers for hayricks.'

There was one rigid airship in commission – the *R32*, which was transferred to the Royal Air Force in 1919. It was then used for experiments by the National Physical Laboratory and for training American crews for the *R38/ZR-2*, before being deleted in 1921.

Britain was also to receive two reparations airships from Germany – the naval Zeppelins *L64* and *L71*, which were delivered to Pulham in June 1920.

There were several rigid airships on order at the end of the war – construction of the *R33* and *R34* had begun in 1917 and they first flew in 1919; *R35*, *R36* and *R37* were the last rigid airships ordered by the Admiralty, but only the *R36* was completed, making its first flight in April 1921. Construction of *R38* started in February 1919, and in October 1919 its sale to the United States was approved by the Cabinet. Work on building the *R80* began in November 1917 – it made its first flight in June 1920 and its last in September 1921.

R33

The *R33* and *R34* were at the design stage in September 1916 when the new Zeppelin *L33* came down at Great Wigborough in Essex. This airship was carefully studied for some months and many of its features were copied for the two British airships. *R33* (built for the Admiralty by Armstrong Whitworth at Barlow, near Selby) was to become the longest-lasting British airship.

Construction work began in the summer of 1917. The frame was made of duralumin and the airship was torpedo-shaped with a blue-grey envelope. It was 670ft long x 80ft diameter, with a capacity of 1,950,000 cubic feet. There were five 250hp Sunbeam Maori engines: one at the rear of the forward gondola, and one in each of the two middle gondolas; the rear gondola carried two engines, which drove one large propeller. *R33* could travel at 60mph.

After test flights in May 1919 the airship appeared over London skies two months later, to publicise the government's new 'Victory Loan', which was an attempt to raise £1,000,000 to pay off debts incurred in the war. It later visited the Midlands and the North, covering 900 miles in thirty-one hours.

In September 1919 the Air Ministry announced that:

> Following upon the conference held on September 8 relating to the Government airship programme, it has been arranged that HM Airship *R33* shall carry out a flight of about thirty-six hours duration in order to demonstrate the capabilities of lighter-than-air craft and as a practical illustration of the comfort afforded to passengers travelling in airships.

The airship, fitted out as a civil airliner, left Pulham at about 8.00 p.m. on 10 September for a flight over some of the First World War battlefields, and a visit to the Amsterdam Aircraft Exhibition. There were ten passengers, including Air Commodore Maitland and Air Ministry officials, the French air attaché and representatives of the Australian government and the Post Office. The chef producing the five-course dinner was from London's Criterion restaurant. A summary of news from *The Times* was sent by wireless from the Marconi station at Wormwood Scrubs, so that passengers could read it while in the air over Amsterdam. *R33* (with *R32*) circled over the exhibition before returning to Britain, landing at Pulham at just after 6.00 p.m.

On the night of 20/21 May 1920 the *R33* took off from Howden carrying an old Sopwith Camel aeroplane. The aim was to test a new type of fire-resistant fuel tank by releasing the pilotless Camel, with engines running, at 1,500ft. The aeroplane crashed into the ground without catching fire.

Just over a year later the *R33* was employed on traffic control duties for the Derby, sending reports by wireless to the deputy commissioner of police, who was in the grandstand at Epsom. Altogether in 1921 the airship made over forty flights from the mooring-mast at Pulham, and stayed at the mast in winds of up to 40mph. In August 1921 *R33* was flown to Cardington and deflated. It would be re-commissioned in 1925.

R34

The *R34* was built by the Beardmore Engineering Company at Inchinnan, near Glasgow, from Admiralty designs influenced by the crashed Zeppelin *L33*. It was 640ft long x 79ft diameter, 1,950,000 cubic feet, with a top speed of 60mph. The framework was made of duralumin, with a keel to support the weight and to provide a gangway (about a foot wide and covered with plywood) for the crew. Below the keel were four gondolas: the front one contained the command area from which navigation was carried out, and ballast and engines were controlled; just behind this was the small wireless cabin.

The front and rear gondolas were on the centre line, and there were also two gondolas 'amidships', one on each side of the hull. The ship was driven by five 250hp Sunbeam Maori engines, with an engine and a propeller at each gondola, except for that at the rear, which had two engines driving one larger propeller.

The intention was for the *R34* to attempt the first flight across the Atlantic, from east to west, to demonstrate the commercial potential. In May 1919 a flying boat of the US Navy captained by Lieutenant-Commander Albert Cushing Read had flown from Newfoundland to the Azores, and then on to Lisbon. The attempt of the *R34* was planned for June 1919 but, because of delays in signing the Peace Treaty, the Admiralty decided not to let the airship go, and sent it instead on a long flight over the coast of Germany. At the end of the fifty-six-hour journey the airship was handed over to the Air Ministry, and overhauled for the Atlantic flight.

Meanwhile, the first non-stop flight across the Atlantic had been made by Captain J. Alcock and Lieutenant Whitten Brown RAF, winning the £10,000 prize put up by the *Daily Mail*. Their flight from Newfoundland to Ireland, in a Vickers Vimy, had taken sixteen hours and twelve minutes.

In preparation for the flight of the *R34*, Colonel Lucas and Major Hugh Fuller had been sent to America as an advance party, and the battle cruisers *Renown* and *Tiger* were stationed in the Atlantic to provide weather reports. According to *The Times* (3 July 1919), Duncan Ewen of Glasgow University gave the officers of the airship some instruction in astronomical observation: 'Two of his appliances have been taken. One of these is an umbrella with a map of the heavens painted inside it, and the other a metal dome, pierced with holes of varying magnitude, so that held against the light it gives an accurate representation of the night sky.'

Captain of the airship was thirty-one-year-old Major George Herbert Scott. Major Scott had trained at the Royal Naval Engineering College at Keyham, and during the First World War had been stationed at Barrow-in-Furness and Anglesey, before being given command of *No.9* – Britain's first rigid airship.

The flight of *R34* began at 2.42 a.m. BST from East Fortune, near North Berwick – destination Roosevelt Field, Mineola, Long Island, New York. Among the thirty-one people on board were Colonel (Acting Brigadier) Edward Maitland, as a representative of the Air Ministry, and Lieutenant Commander Zachary Lansdowne, United States Navy (who was later to command the *Shenandoah*). Next morning Maitland wrote: 'Breakfast, which consisted of cold ham and a hard-boiled egg each, bread and butter, and hot tea. We breakfast in two watches, generally about 15 in each ... in the adjoining compartment was a gramophone entertaining the crew to the latest jazz tunes.' At another point he records that Met. Officer Lieutenant Guy Harris 'unwisely shuts his hand in the door of the wireless cabin. Injury painful, but not serious. Flow of language not audible to me as forward engine happened to be running.'

Another who kept a diary was the engineering officer, Lieutenant John Shotter. Later in the flight he was of the opinion that:

> If in the future an air line is organised between London and New York unless amusements are organised the passengers will be fearfully dull. One can only see at best a vast expanse of sea and at worst fog or an awful downcast sky. Our gramophone is a Godsend to us. I saw four of the crew dancing a sort of rag just now.

Shotter obtained some relief from boredom when he had to repair a cracked cylinder water jacket, which he did with a sheet of copper and some chewing-gum.

As they reached Newfoundland, on 4 July, a message was sent to the wireless station at Cape Race, for onward transmission to the Air Ministry in London: 'Passed over coast near Trinity Bay and proceeding to New York. Passing out from Fortune Bay. Signed, Scott, R34.' The airship came up against electrical storms over Newfoundland and Nova Scotia, which meant that frequent alterations of course had to be made, which in turn led to increased fuel consumption. Lieutenant-Commander Lansdowne signalled from the *R34* to Boston and Washington, requesting that a destroyer be made ready to tow the airship 'if we run out of petrol during the night'. Two hundred men, with petrol and hydrogen, rushed from Mineola to Montauk, at the north end of Long Island but, in the event, *R34* was able to reach Mineola with forty minutes of fuel left.

At Mineola all hotels were full, and many people camped out. A grandstand had been erected at Roosevelt Field. 500 military policemen controlled the crowds and 700 men

67 *R34*, commanded by Major G.H. Scott, arriving at Mineola, Long Island, after the first airship crossing of the Atlantic.

from balloon companies were brought in to handle the airship. Fire engines, ambulances and the Red Cross were all at readiness.

Major John Pritchard parachuted down to supervise operations on the ground, and was taken by motorcycle to the control point. The 3,600-mile flight had taken 108 hours and twelve minutes. Major Scott received a message from King George V: 'Heartiest congratulations to yourself and the crew of *R34* on your splendid achievement, and best wishes for a safe return. Your flight marks the beginning of an era in which the English-speaking peoples, already drawn together in war, will be even more closely united in peace.'

Next day, the airship might have been lost when it became superheated and lifted to an angle of forty-five degrees. In the morning sun the gas temperature had risen above that

68 Major George Herbert Scott on arrival at Mineola.

of the surrounding air, causing the *R34* to rise. It might easily have been blown away, but a mooring shackle had jammed.

The British officers stayed at a hotel as guests of the Aero Club of America; motor cars were available on request. And the airship was presented with a new gramophone and records.

The *New York Times* (*7 July 1919*) told its readers that:

> The *R34* is the pioneer of the air fleets of commerce and pleasure, which in a very few years will make the flight from the New World to the Old, a very brief, luxurious, and compara-tively tame enterprise. The flights of 1919 were gallant adventures; the voyage of the *R34* is the real beginning of a new age.

The plan was that the *R34* would start the homeward journey at dawn on 11 July, but a storm was forecast, so messages were sent to recall Scott and Maitland from a farewell dinner in Garden City. The 400 soldiers of the duty ground crew were turned out, and the airship ascended just before midnight. In spite of the rush, Scott manoeuvred his craft for an hour over New York, where it was illuminated by searchlights and tramcars came to a halt so that passengers could get a better view.

On the return flight an engine broke down, but at 9.10 BST on 12 July *R34* passed over Clifden, Connemara. The Air Ministry was monitoring the flight by wireless, and in the early hours of 13 July the airship was ordered to land at Pulham in Norfolk, rather than at East Fortune in Scotland, because of bad weather. *R34* altered course and flew over the Isle of Man, Liverpool, Derby and Nottingham, before descending at Pulham at 7.56 a.m. after a voyage of seventy-five hours and three minutes. *R34* was the first aircraft to fly from Britain to the United States, and the first to make a return flight across the Atlantic.

Apart from Royal Air Force personnel, not many were there to watch the arrival at Pulham, because of the diversion from East Fortune. An RAF band – depleted because of weekend leave – played *See the Conquering Hero Comes*. The airship was moved into the shed and put on public display alongside *R33*.

Congratulatory messages arrived from the king, the prime minister (David Lloyd George), the secretary of state for air (Winston Churchill), the chief of the air staff (Sir Hugh Trenchard) and the controller-general of civil aviation (Sir Frederick Sykes). Within twenty-four hours cinemas throughout Britain were showing motion pictures of the *R34*'s arrival in New York – the film had been carried to Britain by the airship itself. A month later various awards were gazetted: a CBE to Major Scott, plus nine Air Force Crosses and Air Force Medals to members of the crew.

The airship made a detour over London before returning to East Fortune. Officers and crew were accorded a public welcome in St Andrew's Hall, Glasgow, and were 'entertained at luncheon by Sir William Beardmore, whose firm built the airship'.

Two years later the *R34* was still in commission, and used for training by the Royal Air Force. On 27 January 1921 the airship was on a training flight for navigators, with thirty-two people on board, when the captain became concerned at the deterioration of the weather. Eventually he was able to contact Howden and was told to return. Soon after midnight, at 1,200ft, the airship struck a mountain. With propellers damaged the *R34* was blown out to sea. Sixteen hours later it made it back to Howden. On the ground, 400 men tried to walk the airship into the shed, but the wind made this impossible, so it had to be tethered in the open using a three-wire system. In these conditions it could not be con-trolled and was repeatedly dashed against the ground, causing part of the nose to be ripped off. *R34* never flew again.

R80

The *R80* was designed during the First World War by Barnes Wallis, and built by Vickers: it was 530ft long x 70ft diameter, 1,250,000 cubic feet capacity, and could be armed with a two-pounder gun and several machine-guns, as well as eight 230lb bombs. It was finally handed over to the Royal Air Force in January 1921, subsequently being flown by US Navy crews who were waiting to take delivery of the *R38/ZR-2*. After airtime of only seventy-five hours the *R80* was scrapped in 1924.

GOVERNMENT POLICY

At the beginning of January 1919 a Department of Civil Aviation was formed within the Air Ministry, its first controller-general being Major-General Sir Frederick Sykes, recently chief of the air staff. A memorandum produced for the Air Ministry at this time took the view that the airship should be regarded as a long-distance carrier, compared with the short-range fast aeroplane. 'For commercial purposes large rigid airship stations should be established at distances of 2,000 to 3,000 miles apart, mainly for trans-oceanic traffic, the aeroplane being used for bringing passengers and merchandise to those from the neighbouring countries.'

By the middle of 1919 the government was under increasing pressure to cut public expenditure, and it was announced that all current work on airships would stop, and no more would be built. In September representatives of aviation interests were briefed by the Air Ministry: airships, airship stations, stores and equipment were to be disposed of, and anyone interested was invited to take them over. The Cabinet had decided that the *R38* would go to America, and the under-secretary of state for air, Major-General Seely, announced that 'The US Navy will take over the vessel at cost price, the RAF to undertake the training of American Naval Personnel free of cost, except for pay and rations.'

Commercial firms showed little interest in the proposal that they should acquire the state's airship assets, and by December 1919 a decision had been made that the RAF would retain one rigid and two non-rigid airships for research purposes, together with the base at Howden, in Yorkshire. In April 1920 the Air Ministry's Department of Civil Aviation took over the Short Brothers' facility at Cardington, which became the Royal Airship Works.

The Department of Civil Aviation's plans had developed further by the end of 1920. Its objective was still that the airships be operated by a private company, but it announced that, as a temporary measure, the department would take charge of the airships *R36* and *R37*, and the Zeppelins *L64* and *L71*. The *R33* was being loaned to the RAF. The Department of Civil Aviation would also be responsible for facilities and equipment 'in order to carry out experimental work of an operational character, such as mooring-mast tests and flights of primary importance to gauge the ships' capacity for commercial operation.' The results of this work would be given to any company agreeing to take on the airships.

The headquarters of the Civil Aviation Service would be located at Pulham, with Major E.W. Fuller as Civilian Aviation Traffic Officer and Major G.H. Scott responsible for flying and experimental work. Pulham, near Norwich, had been opened as a Naval Air Station in February 1916. There were two large sheds: No.1 rigid shed was 712ft long x 150ft wide x 100ft high; No.2 shed was larger, and there was also a shed for *Coastal Class* airships. Pulham was the base for the Air Construction Corps.

At the Airship Experimental Station, Pulham had developed an interest in the performance of airships at the mooring-mast, use of which dispensed with the huge squads of men normally needed for landing and ascending. A mast developed by Vickers was 150ft high and constructed of latticed steel. An airship's nose could be attached, with the aid of an electric winch, to the revolving mechanism at the top of the mast. Floating in the air, the craft could swing around with changes in wind direction, like a ship in a current. It was intended that passengers and freight would be taken up the mast in a lift, entering the airship by an enclosed gangway, but the Pulham mast was only 100ft high and had ladders, rather than a lift, and a traction engine instead of an electric winch.

In May 1921 the government made another attempt to get rid of its airships. *The Times* carried the headline 'FREE OFFER OF AIRSHIPS'. The government wished to hand over free to a private company the *R33, R36, R37, R80, L64* and *L71* together with all airship material such as spare engines, fabric, stores and base equipment. It would also pass on all technical information and data gained from experimental work. If firm arrangements had not been made by 1 August 1921, everything would be passed to the Disposal Board.

On 30 June, in the House of Commons, Lieutenant-Commander Kenworthy (MP for Hull Central) asked the secretary of state for air: 'May we take it that in a month's time we shall have finally disposed of these costly luxuries?' Reply: 'Yes, sir; the final date is August 1st.'

Cardington was put up for sale or lease. It was advertised as being three miles from Bedford, with all the facilities necessary to build and repair airships, including an engineering shop, tool room, and shops for working wood, sheet-metal, fabric and for doping. There was a hydrogen plant, an airship shed and a village with housing for 150 families.

Pulham was also for sale or lease: sixteen miles south of Norwich, an operational base with gas and power plants, repair shops, met. office, wireless station, mooring-mast, and two sheds for rigid airships. The huts could accommodate 'several hundred' men.

Conference of Dominion Prime Ministers

As the 'final date' for British airships passed, on 1 August 1921, the dominion prime ministers decided to set up an expert sub-committee to review the future of imperial air communications. The membership of this high-powered committee included: secretary of state for air, under-secretary of state, chief of the air staff, controller-general of civil aviation, and representatives of the Treasury, Colonial Office, India Office, Australia and New Zealand, and South Africa. Its terms of reference were:

> To report (1) on the cost of erecting masts, providing bases and fuel supplies, upkeep of, commissioning and operating the existing fleet of airships for the purpose of Imperial Air Communications with special reference to the routes between England, India, Africa, Australia and New Zealand; and (2) on services by means of aeroplanes.

The sub-committee's conclusions were contained in the official report of the conference (Cmd 1474): an airship service to Egypt, where a base would be built, should begin in March 1922. Six months after that the route could be extended to India. The reparations Zeppelin *L71* would be used, but for a regular service to Egypt, India, South Africa and Australia ten to twelve airships of 4,000,000 cubic feet would be needed, each carrying thirty to thirty-five passengers and two tons of cargo.

The dominion prime ministers decided that the proposals should be put to the governments and parliaments of the empire. Meanwhile, anything necessary for developing imperial air communications should be retained. At the last minute the British airships were reprieved, at least until the dominion parliaments had given their views.

R36/G-FAAF

Because of the government policy of trying to interest private firms, *R36* was fitted out for fifty passengers in twenty-five cabins and registered as civilian aircraft G-FAAF. Built by Beardmore's, the design of the *R36* had been influenced by information acquired from the Zeppelin *L49* which came down in France in October 1917. The airship was 672ft long x 79ft diameter, with a capacity of 2,100,000 cubic feet.

R36 was destined to fly for just under three months. The first trials (commanded by Flight Lieutenant A.H. Wann, with Generals Maitland and Brooke-Popham on board) were held in early April 1921. The *R36* successfully completed a 400-mile trip in fifteen and a half hours, before setting off on its delivery flight to Pulham, via Salisbury Plain and London, damaging rudder and elevator in the process.

Two months later the airship was sent off to test direction-finding capabilities, and the Air Ministry wireless stations at Pulham and Croydon tracked it over Holbeach, King's Lynn, Stafford, Burton-on-Trent, Manchester and Liverpool. Among other flights was that of 14 June, when the *R36* emulated the *R33* by helping the Metropolitan Police to control the road traffic going to a race meeting, this time at Ascot. With the crew of thirty-five there were twenty-five passengers, many of whom were unenthusiastic about the long climb up the access ladder at the Pulham mast. Reports for newspapers, and photographic films, were dropped by parachute over Croydon aerodrome. *The Times* reporter wrote that:

> The case for commercial airships was never more strongly put than by the *R36* in this flight, which is the first in which any section of the public has been asked to travel in a fully-equipped and fitted commercial airship. Travel by lighter-than-air craft is infinitely more enjoyable than travel in an aeroplane, and certainly safer.

A large group of Members of Parliament visited Pulham on 17 June 1921. Travelling by train, they arrived at Pulham St Mary at about 12.30 p.m. They inspected the two reparations Zeppelins, base installations and accommodation, before being taken on a two and a half hour trip in *R36* over Great Yarmouth, Lowestoft and out to sea.

The airship's final flight took place four days later, on 21 June 1921: up to Scarborough, York and back over Lincolnshire to Norfolk. Landing at Pulham at about 9.15 p.m. the bow girders of *R36* were damaged at the mooring-mast and it became necessary to move the airship into the shed straightaway. There was no room, so it was decided that Zeppelin *L64* would have to be sacrificed – within hours it had been roughly dismantled and *R36* was in the shed.

With the future of British airships uncertain, the *R36* was not repaired, but four years later it appeared that it would be employed on a proving flight to Egypt and a new envelope was fitted. In the end, it was realised that the airship was not suitable for the task, and it was dismantled in June 1926.

R38/ZR-2

Following the announcement of the government's proposed 'giveaway' of airships, representatives of the press were invited to Cardington, in early June 1921, to inspect the new *R38* being built for the United States Navy (as *ZR-2*).

R38, the largest airship yet built, was designed by the Admiralty, begun by Short Brothers, and finished by the Air Ministry. The design work had been done by the Admiralty early in 1918, and Short Brothers began construction in November 1918. In October 1919 the Cabinet approved the sale to the United States. In April 1920 Shorts' Cardington works was taken over by the government.

The airship was 695ft long x 85ft, with a capacity of 2,700,000 cubic feet. There were six 350hp Sunbeam Cossack engines, and endurance at 60mph was 6,500 miles. The framework was of duralumin with a corridor, running the length of the ship, along which were the crew's accommodation, aluminium petrol tanks, and bomb racks.

The first flight was on 23 June 1921 when it was flown from Cardington to Howden. The fourth, and last, flight came two months later. On the night of 23/24 August 1921, the *R38*, on a test flight, stayed out over the sea. Next day more manoeuvres took place, including turning trials. During one of these the airship crumpled in the middle, and there were two explosions. The *R38* fell into the Humber off Hull, with much of the forward part destroyed by fire. Forty-four were killed, including sixteen Americans; five men in the rear section survived: the captain, three crew members and one man from the National Physical Laboratory.

The Report of the Accident Investigating Sub-Committee concluded that the disaster was caused by structural weakness in the design of the airship – 'having regard to her size and speed, *R38* was considerably weaker than previous British rigid airships.'

A monument unveiled at Hull in 1924 has the names of the dead and the inscription:

To the glory of God and in memory of the officers and men of the Royal Air Force and of the Rigid Air Detachment, United States Navy, members of the staffs of the National Physical Laboratory and of the Royal Airship Works, lost in the airship *R38* (*ZR2*), August 24, 1921.

69 The first flight of the *R38/US Navy ZR-2* was on 23 June 1921, when it was flown from Cardington to Howden.

70 *R38/ZR-2* being walked out of the shed at Howden, June–August 1921.

71 The wreckage of the *R38/ZR-2* in the Humber, 24 August 1921. Forty-four men died.

There was an RAF guard of honour, the last post and reveille were sounded, and the two national anthems were sung.

THE BURNEY SCHEME

Charles Dennistoun Burney (1888–1968) was a naval officer who developed an interest in aviation. He retired from the service in 1920 as a lieutenant-commander and two years later became MP for Uxbridge. Associated with Vickers, he became a prominent advocate of the use of airships, writing in 1929 that the employment of airships would:

> Shorten the distances that separate the various parts of the imperial system … weld it into a
> solid economic and political structure, and so give it sufficient power such as will enable the
> Empire to compete on level terms with a continental organisation like the United States …
> The future of the Empire lies in the air. It is no exaggeration to say that not only its political
> and economic development but also its continued existence depend on our capacity to estab-
> lish within the next generation an efficient system of Imperial communications.

Burney's proposal, submitted to the Air Ministry in August 1922 was to: firstly, develop an airship which could reach India in 100 flying hours (a sea voyage took six weeks), starting with a trial service between Britain and Egypt; secondly, provide a weekly service to India with more than one airship; then increase the frequency of service and, eventually, run six large (5,000,000 cubic feet) airships.

At the Imperial Conference of October 1923 the Conservative secretary of state for air (Sir Samuel Hoare) announced that his government had, in principle, accepted the Burney scheme, and would provide financial assistance. Next month Vickers and Dennistoun Burney formed the Airship Guarantee Company. Two months after that there was a change of government.

The first Labour government came into power on 22 January 1924 as a minority admin- istration: Labour had 191 seats, Conservatives 258, so Labour had to rely on the support of the Liberals. The new secretary of state for air was Christopher Birdwood Thomson who, like his father and father-in-law, had been an army officer. His service in the Royal Engineers took him to Mashonaland, Mauritius, South Africa and Serbia. In the First World War Thomson was in Belgium, Romania and Palestine before being made a member of the British delegation at the Peace Conference. He left the army in 1919, joined the Labour party and tried, unsuccessfully, to be elected to parliament. He was made Baron Thomson of Cardington, so that he could sit in the House of Lords.

In April 1924 the new government encouraged the formation of Imperial Airways, which began with a dozen aeroplanes and a government subsidy. At the same time a cabinet committee was set up to re-examine the Burney scheme for airship operations.

A month later (21 May 1924) Lord Thomson announced the cabinet committee's con- clusions in the House of Lords. He first gave an outline of the Burney scheme accepted by the previous government and its demands on the public purse: (1) over the first seven years a total of £2,800,000 would be paid. For this, six airships would be built, remain- ing the property of the company which built them. (2) For the next eight years another £2,000,000 would be payable in fees – 'For this sum six airships would be operated on the Indian route, but those ships would only be available for other purposes in return for spe- cial charter rates'. (3) During the period of the agreement (fifteen years) the total payable from public funds would be £4,800,000; in addition, the company would have free use of 'the valuable properties at Cardington and Pulham' with all their machinery and plant. (4) The Burney scheme proposed that half of the company's net profits each year would be put by to repay the subsidies, providing non-interest-bearing debentures as security. It was estimated that it would take at least sixty years to repay the total amount, and that was assuming profits averaging twenty per cent. Lord Thomson concluded that at the end of fifteen years the company would have a virtual monopoly:

> In view of the immense sums of public money with which it had been endowed, and its pos-session of the unique stations at Cardington and Pulham … the company would have become, under the original agreement, almost a State Department – disposing of these enormous sums merely on the fulfilment of not very onerous conditions.

Thomson went on:

> Justice, however, demanded that he should refer to the advantages of the Burney scheme. Under its provisions there might have been a fleet of six airships within seven to fourteen years, and the presumption was that a not inconsiderable sum of private money staked in the enterprise might have served as an incentive to energetic effort. The enthusiastic optimism of Commander Burney had been remarkable. He had kept alive interest in airship development when others doubted.

But Lord Thomson felt that Commander Burney was naturally inclined to see the prospects of the company 'through the rose-tinted spectacles of a man who, for the moment, was a company promoter.' Airships had not properly been tried out, and their safety had not been proved. Until they had been, they were not likely to be of much commercial value.

THE GOVERNMENT SCHEME

Lord Thomson then outlined the Labour government's proposals, which envisaged an initial three-year programme, with net public expenditure of under £1,200,000. It was stressed that the whole scheme was experimental, with the aim of examining the possible use of airships as a means of long-distance transport.

The Air Ministry would:

(1) be responsible for research, including experimental flights with one of the existing airships, which would be reconditioned. (After the *R38* disaster, less than three years before, in which forty-four men died and the *Dixmude* tragedy only five months ear-lier, in which fifty men died, the British government and its advisers were well aware of the importance of an effective programme of research and development.)
(2) build a 5,000,000 cubic feet airship at Cardington. The design was to take into account possible military roles, including naval reconnaissance.
(3) provide the necessary ground installations in Britain, India and places in between.

As to the role of private firms:

(1) If satisfactory terms could be agreed, the Air Ministry would place a contract 'with the interest represented by Commander Burney' for an airship of 5,000,000 cubic feet, intended for civilian uses.

(2) Results from the Air Ministry's programme of research would be given to Commander
    Burney. 'These proposals should enable two airships to be placed in commission in a
    shorter period than under the original scheme. The government ship and the com-
    mercial ship will be laid down simultaneously.'

There would be two new advisory boards. One would 'deal with the proper aspects of
airship development', and would include representatives of the Treasury, Admiralty, War
Office, Air Ministry, Colonial Office and Post Office.

The second, a 'technical' board, was to be 'the consultant body for the construction of
both ships' with representatives from the Admiralty, War Officeand Air Ministry, together
with outside experts.

A Directorate of Airship Development was established as part of the Air Ministry – Director:
Group Captain P.F.M. Fellowes, DSO; Deputy Director: Squadron Leader R.B.B. Colmore
(formerly attached to the Directorate of Civil Aviation for Airships); Superintendent of
Flying Operations: Major G.H. Scott as the superintendent of flying operations; in charge of
construction: Mr H.B.W. Evans (Royal Corps of Naval Constructors); Officer i/c research
and design: Colonel Victor Richmond; Cardington works manager: Mr R.F. Hubbard (formerly of Beardmore's).

Group Captain Fellowes visited India early in 1925 to choose a site for an airship base.
Karachi was selected: the base, and the Ismailia–Karachi route, were to be subsidised by the
British and Indian governments. The shed built at Karachi in 1927 was 850ft long, 180ft
wide and 170ft high, and would be in existence until 1960. The Karachi mast would be
similar to that at Cardington, but with an octagonal building round the foot, and there
would be a ground staff of 150.

The intermediate base at Ismailia would also have a 'Cardington' mast (it was erected in
1926) with buildings to accommodate passengers and crew.

As part of the programme of research required by the airship programme, the National
Physical Laboratory carried out experiments in wind tunnels to find the most efficient
shape for a new airship, and studied the size and shape of fins. A good deal of work was
done on the strength of girders, and the stresses to which they might be subjected.

R33/FAAG

As part of the research programme *R33* was refurbished to fly as an experimental airship
to test recently formulated theories and obtain data. Nearly four years after it last flew the
R33 was walked out of the shed at Cardington (on 2 April 1925) by 300 men. Commanded
by Flight Lieutenant Irwin, with Major Scott on board, the airship flew for two hours
before setting off for Pulham, where it was moored to the mast.

On 14/15 April a gale blew up, with the airship riding at the mast. Major Scott
decided, as a precaution, to put a crew on board, with fuel and provisions for forty-eight
hours. Just before 10.00 a.m. the arm at the top of the mast broke and *R33* was torn away
carrying part of the arm with it. The bows were badly damaged and a gas bag torn. The
first officer of the airship, Flight Lieutenant Ralph S. Booth, and twenty men were on
board.

Flight Lieutenant Booth recorded in the log: 'I investigated the damage done to the
bow more fully. This necessitated a trip to the roof of the ship. We made a bulkhead of the
deflated No.1 gas bag, and this prevented more damage by the gale.' The airship was blown
out over the North Sea as far as the Dutch coast, but there were no airship facilities and to
land would have meant the loss of the ship.

Throughout, the *R33* was in wireless contact with Pulham, and direction-finding stations were able to determine its position, which was passed to the airship, together with weather information. In the late evening of 16 April an attempt was made to return. Slow progress was made, but by 1.00 p.m. on 17th the Suffolk coast had been reached. By 3.00 p.m. the *R33* was over Pulham, with bows 'looking as if they had been hit by a wall'. At 4.00 p.m. the airship was safely in its shed.

It took four months to repair the *R33*. Parts for a new duralumin nose-cone, 35ft long, were made at Cardington and assembled at Pulham. The airship flew again on 5 October 1925, leaving at about 5.00 p.m. for the east coast, Margate, across Kent and over London, returning to Pulham (in spite of gear-box trouble) at about midday. On board were Major Scott, Flight Lieutenant Irwin and Colonel Richmond, who was in charge of the experimental work. Altogether there were forty people, including eight who were studying the external pressure on the hull, using photographs which were developed in the airship's darkroom.

The *R33* also acted as an aircraft carrier. On 15 October 1925 a DH53 was launched from the airship in flight. Piloted by Squadron Leader Rollo Haigh, an aeroplane propeller blade was smashed in attempting to return to the trapeze, but the aircraft was able to glide down to earth. Another trial was made during a flight on 4 December: Rollo Haigh climbed down from the airship (which was commanded by Major Scott) to the DH3, and the trapeze was let down until the aeroplane was about 50ft clear. At that point the pilot pulled the release lever and the aeroplane dropped away. The reverse operation was also successful, and Squadron Leader Haigh was able to climb back into the airship.

72 *R33* arriving at Pulham at 3.00 p.m. on 17 April 1925, with bows 'looking as if they had been hit by a wall'. The airship had been torn away from the mooring mast and blown as far as the Dutch coast. It was eighteen months before the *R33* flew again.

Nearly a year later, on 21 October 1926, the *R33* took to the air with two Gloster Grebes, each weighing over a ton, slung underneath. They were reached by rope ladder from the airship, which was again commanded by Major Scott. The aim was to release both over Pulham, but the engine of one failed to start, so only Flying Officer Mackenzie-Richards could be dropped off. The *R33* carried on to Cardington where Flying Officer Ragg, with the Grebe's engine now working, was able to release his aircraft. The airship landed, and was moved into the hangar where it was to stay until the visit of the dominion prime ministers.

The inspection was made on 17 November 1926. The delegates were attending the Imperial Conference in London, and had a great interest in the progress of the two new airships being built at Howden and Cardington. Journey times to their countries would be vastly decreased: Australia could be reached in twelve and a half days, South Africa in six days, India in five days and Canada in two and a half days. The dominion visitors were told that the Cardington airship would be ready at the end of 1927 or the beginning of 1928. (It would be, in fact, October 1930.)

A week later the *R33* moved from the shed to the new mooring-mast. The airship again had the two Grebe aeroplanes attached underneath. After leaving the mast, the airship gained height before dropping a parachute with a dummy and then one of the aeroplanes. The second Grebe was released at Pulham, where the airship was moved into the hangar, to be laid up. For the next three years there was no British airship flying.

The government's programme required that the two airships – one built by a commercial firm, the other by the Royal Airship Factory – would be constructed using materials and processes developed during the research and experimental phase. The specifications to be met included: Capacity to be 5,000,000 cubic feet, twice the size of any previous British airship; weight, including engines, to be not more than ninety tons, with a useful lift of sixty tons; accommodation for 100 passengers; a cruising speed of 63mph, with a top speed of 70mph. The safety criteria laid down by the Aeronautical Research Committee had to be met, and the engines were to use a fuel approved for use in hot climates – in practice this meant the installation of diesel engines.

R100/G-FAAV

In November 1924 the order for the 'commercially-built' airship was given to the Airship Guarantee Company, whose chairman was Sir Trevor Dawson (vice-chairman of Vickers);. the managing director was Dennistoun Burney. The contract for the *R100*, civilian registration *G-FAAV*, stipulated that the airship should be delivered to the Air Ministry in September 1927. The Airship Guarantee Company had an option to buy the airship back for £150,000.

Design work on the *R100* began at Vickers House in Crayford under the direction of Barnes Wallis who had designed *R90* and *R80* and who would go on to design the Wellington bomber and the 'bouncing' bomb. Chief calculator was Nevil Shute Norway, who was responsible for a team calculating the likely stresses on the airship. He became deputy chief engineeer in 1929, and in his spare time he wrote novels under the name 'Nevil Shute'. The vital basic work went on for eighteen months, including the testing of novel girder designs at Birmingham University.

Components were made by Vickers, and the airship was assembled at Howden, where the airship construction workers arrived in 1926. This Yorkshire base had passed through several hands and the current owner was in the process of dismantling it, removing anything that could be sold. The power house did not work, and the gas plant had gone. The shed covered an area of over seven acres, but it was not in good condition and the damp atmosphere inside could cause airship components to corrode. During construction the decision was taken to treat the airship's girders with anti-corrosion varnish, a job which kept thirty men employed for three months. The gasbags were made by B.G. Textilwerke of Berlin, and the gas valves were bought from the Zeppelin Company.

The airship's length was 709ft, maximum diameter 133ft. With a maximum speed of 80mph, it had a range of 3,500 to 5,000 miles. The capacity was 5,000,000 cubic feet.

The passenger accommodation was on two levels within the hull – there were eighteen four-berth and fourteen two-berth cabins, separated from each other by fabric partitions. On the lower level there was a large dining room, and a promenade deck. The control car was below the hull.

It was originally intended to design a new engine, which would run on a mixture of kerosene and hydrogen, but after a year this idea was dropped. The plan now was to install diesel engines, but this also came to nothing. In the end, six 670hp Rolls-Royce Condor IIIB engines were fitted – there were three power gondolas, with two engines in each. These Rolls-Royce engines ran on petrol, which meant that the *R100* could not be used on flights to India.

In 1927 an 'Airship Mission' from Britain toured Africa, Australia, New Zealand and India. Its members were Group Captain P.F.M. Fellowes (director of airship development), M.A. Giblett (superintendent, airships' meteorological division) and Flight Lieutenant S. Nixon (Royal Airship Works). They inspected possible bases and met government representatives, politicians and local businessmen.

On their return, *Flight* (12 January 1928) reported that 'a provisional skeleton of the chief commercial routes has been prepared' – from Britain to (a) Canada or Newfoundland; (b) Cape Town, either via Cairo and Aden or via the west coast of Africa; (c) India and Ceylon (Sri Lanka) via Cairo and Karachi; (d) to Australia and New Zealand via India and the Cocos Islands or via Africa. It was expected that the first proving flights in the new British airships would be at the end of 1929 or early in 1930, the first being to Canada, but it was again stressed that 'the actual programme for the future necessarily depends upon the exhaustive series of trials which have first to be carried out at home with the new airships.'

Lift and trim trials of the *R100* were begun in November 1929 and on 15 December Major Scott arrived from Cardingon – he was in charge of flying both *R100* and *R101*. Next day the *R100* was walked out at Howden by 400 soldiers. It flew for five hours and forty-seven minutes, circling over York before making for Cardington. There followed seven months of test flights. On 17 December 1929 there was a local flight of six hours and twenty-nine minutes. On 16 January 1930: Grantham and Spalding, thirteen hours and six minutes. 20 January: London area, seven hours and eighteen minutes. 29 January: Southwest England and the Channel Islands, fifty-three hours and fifty-two minutes (1,780 miles). 22 May: Hull and back, twenty-two hours and fifty minutes. 25/26 July: Midlands, Wales and the Channel Islands, twenty-four hours and sixteen minutes. After this last flight the *R100* was formally taken over by the Air Ministry.

Three days later the airship left for Canada. This was to be the second flight of a British airship across the Atlantic, the previous one being that of the *R34* in July 1919.

The Air Ministry informed the press that it was to be an experimental flight, part of the programme to try out airships over long distances, and the results would help in the making of decisions about air links between British Commonwealth countries.

This, only the eighth flight of Air Ministry airship *R100*, was to begin at the Royal Airship Works, Cardington, and end at the St Hubert Air Station, Montreal. The captain was Squadron Leader R.S. Booth AFC, and the navigator Squadron Leader E.L.

Johnston OBE, AFC. There were forty-three on board – thirty-seven crew and six passengers: Wing Commander R.B.B. Colmore (director of airship development), Major G.H. Scott and Mr. F.M. McWade (resident inspector at Cardington for the Aeronautical Inspection Department). Sir Dennistoun Burney and Mr N.S. Norway represented the builders. Lieutenant-Commander R. St J. Prentice represented the Admiralty. The crew members were all civilian, apart from two officers and an NCO seconded from the Royal Air Force.

The *R100* ascended from Cardington at 2.48 a.m. on 29 July 1930. Over the St Lawrence three of the fins were damaged by wind, and the engines had to be stopped for eight hours so that repairs could be made. There was more damage to fins as the airship neared Montreal. The arrival at the St Hubert mast was on 1 August, after seventy-eight hours and forty-nine minutes (and 3,364 miles).

The 60ft-high St Hubert mast had been completed by Canadian Vickers in May. A handling team from the Royal Canadian Navy had been trained at Cardington, and 600 servicemen were mustered to control the thousands of spectators.

Ten days later the *R100* took off on a twenty-six-hour sight-seeing trip for eighteen passengers (army officers, government officials and a journalist) over Ottawa, Toronto, Niagara Falls, and into New York State. As the airship approached the mooring tower on its return a propeller was damaged.

The flight back to England began on 13 August and was accomplished with one engine out of action. There were thirteen passengers, including nine journalists. The fifty-six-hour journey ended at Cardington at 11.06 a.m. on 16 August.

Within two months, the companion airship *R101* had crashed, and the whole imperial airship scheme was called into question. In August 1931 a National government was formed 'to deal with the national emergency that now exists', and to balance the budget. On 15 September there was a naval mutiny at Invergordon in protest at pay cuts, and a week later Britain abandoned the gold standard. In dire economic conditions the axe was taken to public expenditure. All staff concerned with the *R100* were given notice and the airship itself was sold in November 1931 to Elton, Levy & Co., London metal merchants.

Four years later the Airship Guarantee Company was wound up.

R101

The *R101* was to be built at Cardington which meant that the Royal Airship Works – which was in a state of 'care and maintenance' – had to be reopened. The shed was enlarged between 1924 and 1926 and an octagonal mooring-mast, 200ft high, was erected. Passengers were taken up 170ft by lift to the embarkation platform, and then boarded the airship by means of a gangway. At the top of the mast was a telescopic arm, to which the airship moored. In 1928 the No.2 airship shed at Pulham was dismantled, lengthened, and re-erected at Cardington as No.2 shed.

The *R101* design team was led by Colonel Victor Richmond (assistant director of airship development – technical), and the chief calculator was Harold Roxbee Cox, who was engaged on aerodynamics research at Imperial College.

The *Report of the R101 Inquiry* pointed out that 'the designers broke away almost completely from conventional methods and in every direction an attempt was made to improve upon standard Zeppelin practice.' Areas of innovation included the airship's framework, gasbag wiring and valves, control systems and engines. Work on the structure was contracted-out to Boulton & Paul of Norwich, who made components at their Riverside Works and sent them to Cardington for assembly. Parts were tested thoroughly, and about a hundred girders

73 The airship sheds at Cardington. No.1 shed was built during the First World War. No.2 shed was originally at Pulham. It was re-erected at Cardington, and lengthened in 1928.

were tested to destruction. A complete section of the airship, including gas container, was built at Cardington so that experiments could be made to simulate flight stresses.

Ultimately, the airship contained seventeen gasbags, made of cotton lined with goldbeaters' skin. The biggest of these when inflated was 126ft from top to bottom. The wiring of the gasbags employed a new method, which had been patented in 1927 by Colonel Richmond and Squadron Leader Rope. In addition, the relief valves were of a new design.

Dope was put on the envelope's fabric *before* it was put on the airship. The fabric shrank, because of moisture, and long rents appeared which meant that the fabric had to be replaced, and then doped.

A new way of operating the rudder and elevator flaps had been invented by Squadron Leader Rope.

The *Report* concluded that:

> The only effective security against the risk of trying many new experiments in design simultaneously is a prolonged series of trials designed to test out the airworthiness of each new feature in turn. During construction, and in the early trial flights of the *R101*, this policy of cautious experiment at each step was admirably fulfilled.

Experiments and calculations went on for more than two years before components began to be assembled at Cardington. In March 1926 *The Times* was impressed:

> It is not generally known that Great Britain has broken away completely from the Zeppelin tradition of the past. As a result of the scientific study of all the failures and limitations of the war-time ships, together with much original research into problems only partly understood

at the end of the war, this country today is probably leading the world in its knowledge of the underlying principles of airship construction and their practical application. The older forms of continuous lattice work girder, with its complicated assemblies, have been abandoned in favour of steel girders which can be bolted up in the ship. In almost every respect the new State airship shows big constructional advances.

The original dimensions of the ship were: 730ft long x 130ft maximum diameter, 4,893,740 cubic feet capacity, with a maximum speed of 70mph and an endurance of forty-two hours. There was a crew of forty-eight. The main passenger lounge measured 60ft x 32ft and was positioned across the width of the hull, with a promenade at each end. The dining room could seat fifty people, and there was a 'fire-proof' smoking room.

The government's specifications included the requirement that, because of the proposed flights to India, a less volatile fuel than petrol should be used. Five 585hp Beardmore Tornado engines were installed, but these were very heavy – a total of eighteen tons. (The Rolls-Royce engines on the *R100* weighed under eleven tons.)

On 30 September 1929 the gasbags were filled and lift and trim tests were carried out, but instead of an expected useful lift of ninety tons, it was only about thirty-five tons, which meant that the airship could not be employed on the route to India.

Twelve days later the *R101* was moved from shed to mooring-mast. *The Times* of 14 October 1929:

> One million people travelled from all parts of the country to gaze in awe at the giant silver airship as she went through her final trials at the mooring-mast today ... the scenes at the air station were unequalled in the history of airship flying. Battalions of police, stationed every hundred yards along four miles of roadway leading to Cardington, were powerless to deal with the congestion. Hundreds of omnibuses arrived here all day, travelling from Newcastle, Leeds, Cardiff, Swansea and Nottingham ... The predominant impression made by the State Airship *R101*, as she now swings at the masthead at the Royal Airship Works, silver in colour and imposing in size, is the way she looks right and in a way in which the elongated cigar ships of the War period never did.

The first flight was around London for five hours and thirty-eight minutes, using only two engines. Four engines powered the second flight (the fifth engine was still a reversing-engine only) over the Midland counties for nine hours and thirty-eight minutes on 18 October. Lord Thomson was on board.

Three days later a storm was forecast which drove the *R101* back into the Cardington shed for ten days.

The airship made seven flights in November: on the 1st it went to Wisbech and King's Lynn, then passed twice over Sandringham before continuing to Sheringham and Cromer. Norwich was next, where *R101* flew over Boulton & Paul's works. Then to Pulham, Diss, Bury St Edmunds, Newmarket and Cambridge – making a total of seven hours and fifteen minutes. The fourth ascent, the first at night, was on 2/3 November and took the airship towards the Isle of Wight. The flight lasted for fourteen hours two minutes; one engine failed. The next two flights were local, each for just over three hours.

The final flight in November was to be an endurance test, including turning trials – it was to be of at least thirty-six hours and if possible forty-eight hours. In fact it lasted for thirty hours and forty-one minutes, from 10.30 a.m. on 17 November until 5.00 p.m. on the next day – over England, Scotland and Ireland at 1,000 to 1,500ft.

74 *R101* was built at the Royal Airship Works at Cardington. Its original dimensions were: 730 feet long x 130ft diameter and 4,893,740 cubic feet capacity. The first flight, which attracted thousands of spectators, was made in October 1929.

At the end of November the *R101* went into its shed for seven months to undergo a weight reduction programme in order to increase the useful lift. Twelve passenger cabins were taken out, as were two lavatories, two water-ballast tanks and the heavy glass in the windows of the promenade. Also to disappear were the lookout position on top of the airship and the servo equipment which assisted steering. Adjustments were made to the wires supporting the gasbags, which could then hold more hydrogen.

During this period it was found that all the gasbags had holes, caused by chafing on the framework, so 4,000 pads were fitted to stop the same thing happening again.

The *R101* emerged into the open air on 2 June 1930, when it was moored at the Cardington mast to be made ready for an appearance at the Royal Air Force Display at Hendon. A split about 140ft long appeared on the starboard side of the envelope, which meant that men had to work on it all day, in wind and rain. Next day another gash had to be mended, and it was decided to reinforce the envelope with bands of fabric. The cover was tested in a flight of four hours and thirty-five minutes on 26 June – the airship's eighth flight. The ninth flight was a rehearsal for the display, and the *R101* flew over London, then over Hendon airfield. Test transmissions of weather maps were sent by wireless from the meteorological station at Cardington. The airship was back over its base by 3.00 p.m., but cruised around locally for five and a half hours, making a total airtime of twelve hours and thirty-three minutes. The Royal Air Force Display took place at Hendon next day, 28 June, when a crowd of 150,000 saw the display of the *R101*.

Then it was back into the Cardington shed. After the previous seven month's sojourn, the airship had been out of the shed for just six days, and now it was back inside for another three months. This time the airship was to be rebuilt, with a new bay being fitted between frames eight and nine, and a new gasbag, larger than the existing ones.

A test flight of the rebuilt airship began in perfect weather at 4.30 p.m. on 1 October 1930. The original plan had been to stay airborne for forty-eight hours, but this was reduced to twenty-four. The actual length of the flight was sixteen hours and fifty-one minutes, during which time the airship flew over London, Southend, the North Sea, Great Yarmouth and back to Cardington. No speed trials were conducted, and there was trouble with the oil cooler of one of the engines. A certificate of airworthiness was issued after the flight 'as soon as the Inspection Department of the Ministry was satisfied' (*Report of the R101 Inquiry*).

In the Air Ministry Wing Commander Colmore had obtained the agreement of the air member for supply and research (Air Vice-Marshal Dowding) that, if no major problems arose, the test flight would be shorter than planned. If this was done, the flight to India could set off within the next two days. The decision to attempt this hurried departure was made because of the desire to fly the secretary of state for air to India and back before the end of the Imperial Conference, which was being held in London. (There were contingency plans to bring Lord Thomson back by aeroplane if necessary). *The Report of the R101 Inquiry* took the view that 'The trials of the reconstructed ship were cut down to a degree that would never have been thought proper if it had not been for the exigencies of time.'

In the *Manchester Guardian* Major F.A. De V. Robertson wrote:

> Tomorrow evening the airship *R101* will start from Cardington for Ismailia, en route for Karachi. The Air Minister, Lord Thomson, and the Director of Civil Aviation, Sir Sefton Brancker, will be on board, but no private passengers or journalists. The flight is a greater and more interesting experiment than the flight of *R100* to Canada. *R101* embodies more experimental features than *R100*, and this flight will take an airship into tropical climes … There seems a future prospect that passengers to India and Australia will go by airship, but for the present we must be content to learn what the *R101* can teach us by her maiden flight to Karachi.

The journey to India began on the evening of 4 October 1930, with fifty-four people on board. Captain was Flight Lieutenant H.C. Irwin; navigator Squadron Leader E.L. Johnston; first officer Lieutenant-Commander N.G. Atherstone; second officer Flying Officer M.H. Steff; and met. officer Maurice Giblett. There were thirty-seven crew members. The officer in charge of the flight was Major Scott (assistant director of airship development – flying). Others on board were: Wing Commander Colmore (director of airship development), Colonel Richmond (assistant director of airship development – technical), Squadron

Leader Rope (assistant to Colonel Richmond), Mr A. Bushfield (Aeronautical Inspection Department) and Mr H.J. Leech (foreman engineer, Cardington).

Then there were: Lord Thomson (secretary of state for air), Sir Sefton Brancker (director of civil aviation), Major Bishop (chief inspector, aeronautical inspection department), Squadron Leader Palstra (Australian liaison officer), Squadron Leader O'Neill (deputy director of civil aviation) and James Buck (Lord Thomson's valet).

As the *R101* passed over London those on board were able to listen to a special programme broadcast by the BBC Dance Band. Later, the engine in the rear car was found to be playing up, but it was working again as the airship reached France.

Just after midnight Cardington received a message which ended:'After an excellent supper our distinguished passengers smoked a final cigar and having sighted the French coast have now gone to bed to rest after the excitement of their leave-taking. All essential services are functioning satisfactorily. The crew have settled down to watch-keeping routine.'

At 1.51 a.m. the Le Bourget wireless station fixed the airship's position as being near Beauvais. At 2.05 a.m., in a forty to 50mph gusting wind, the nose dropped, and for about half a minute the *R101* went into a steep dive. This was controlled by use of the elevator but, almost immediately, the airship dived again. This time it hit the ground, although the crash was described as 'not severe'. *R101* ploughed along the ground for about twenty yards, before bursting into flames. Of the fifty-four people on board, forty-six were killed and two died the next day. Six men survived: A. Disley, A.V. Bell, J.H. Binks, A.J. Cook, V. Savory and H.J. Leech.

The funeral of the victims took place in London on 13 October 1930. Tens of thousands visited the lying-in-state at Westminster Hall before the coffins were brought out for the procession, the route lined with silent crowds. First came the mounted police followed by a Royal Air Force detachment. The wreaths from the royal family and the Air Council came next, and twenty-four wagons each bearing a coffin. After these were the Grenadier

75 The *R101* crashed near Beauvais in northern France in the early hours of 5 October 1930. It was on its way to India. Of the fifty-four people on board, six survived.

Guards, the band of the Welsh Guards and then the other twenty-four coffins. In attend-
ance were the prime minister and cabinet, and representatives of the dominions and foreign
countries. The cortège wound its way up Whitehall, through Trafalgar Square, along the
Strand and Aldwych into Kingsway, past the Air Ministry. The coffins were placed on a
special train at Euston, to be taken to a common grave at Cardington.

Why did the *R101* crash? A public inquiry was held by Sir John Simon, with Lieutenant-
Colonel J.T.C. Moore-Brabazon and Professor C.E. Inglis as assessors. They reached the
unanimous conclusion that 'the immediate cause of the disaster was leakage culminating
in a substantial loss of gas from one or more bags in the fore part of the ship.' They thought
that 'the most probable cause of a deflated gasbag is the buffeting it would receive in
consequence of a tear in the outer cover.' As for the fire, 'If a spark caused by the broken
electric circuit reached a mixture of hydrogen-gas and air it would instantly set the mixture on fire, though the force of the immediate explosion would vary with the proportions
of the mixture. This seems, therefore, to be the most probable cause of the fire.' The report
pointed out that the rebuilt *R101* left for India after a test flight of just under sixteen hours,
which had been made in perfect weather:

> It is clear that if those responsible had been entirely free to choose the time and the weather
> in which the *R101* should start for the first flight ever undertaken by any airship to India, and
> if the only considerations governing their choice were considerations of meteorology and of
> preparation for the voyage, the *R101* would not have started when she did.

The whole airship programme was cancelled, including plans for building airships *R102*,
R103 and *R104*.

UNITED STATES

Commercial Airships

After the First World War the Goodyear Tire and Rubber Company began to build and
operate non-rigid airships – blimps – for pleasure flights and for advertising.

The *Wingfoot Express* promoted Goodyear's Wingfoot road haulage business, which began
on 9 April 1919. The airship, which could carry eight passengers, was 186ft long and powered
by two 80hp Gnome rotary engines. The Goodyear hangars at Akron were still occupied by
the army, so the *Wingfoot Express* test flights set off from the White City, Chicago.

The maiden flight was on 21 July 1919. On the second ascent, on the same day, pilot
Jack Boettner took up two army officers, Colonel Joseph Morrow and Major Clarence
Moranville. On the third flight that day the *Wingfoot Express* burst into flames over Chicago,
dropping through the glass roof of the Illinois Trust and Savings Bank, where 200 people
were at work. The airship's petrol tanks exploded, killing eight and badly injuring twenty-
seven. Of the men on the airship, three were killed and two came down by parachute.

Jack Boettner:

> We were at least 1,200ft above the ground when I first felt the heat of the flames. Looking
> back, I saw fire on both sides of the bag. I watched the flames for a couple of seconds before I
> said anything to the other fellows. Knowing that the ship was finished I shouted 'over the top,

everybody!' As I yelled, I felt the frame buckle, but by this time they were beginning to slide over the sides … I saw one of the parachutes on fire.

Boettner landed on top of a building, and then came down the fire escape.

Three small non-rigids built by Goodyear in 1919-20 were known as *Pony Blimps*. They were 95ft long x 28ft maximum diameter, and 35,350 cubic feet. Powered by a Lawrence 50hp engine, the blimp could reach 45mph. One was bought by the Commercial Airship Syndicate, formed in 1919 at Kansas City; this craft was destroyed, with its shed, by gale-force winds. Another went to provide pleasure trips between Long Beach and Catalina Island, California. The third *Pony Blimp* was destroyed by fire, along with the navy's *D-1*, on 19 July 1920, in Goodyear's hangar at Akron.

Pilgrim

Pilgrim was the first of a series of small blimps built by Goodyear. The British journal *Flight* called it 'an interesting little sporting airship'. It was 110ft long x 31ft diameter with a cubic capacity of 53,000 cubic feet of helium. A Lawrence 60hp air-cooled engine mounted on the gondola produced a top speed of 50mph; the range was 500 miles. Although usually called a 'non-rigid' there was an internal keel, made of steel tubes coated in magnesium. In addition to a crew of two there was room for two passengers. A novel feature was that the airship had its own portable mooring-mast. The first ascent was on 3 June 1925, and the *Pilgrim* was to fly for more than 2,800 hours, carrying 5,350 passengers, before being taken out of service in December 1931.

In 1928 the *Puritan* was produced by Goodyear-Zeppelin under the direction of Karl Arnstein, former chief engineer of the German Zeppelin Company, and now the vice-president of the American company. *Puritan* was a larger and improved version of the *Pilgrim*, being 128ft long x 37ft diameter, with a capacity of 86,000 cubic feet and a top speed of 55mph. There were two air-cooled radial engines mounted on outriggers at the rear of the gondola, which was enclosed and could accommodate up to six passengers.

The airships in the Goodyear series of advertising blimps were nearly all named after winners of the America's Cup sailing competition: after *Puritan*, in 1929, came *Volunteer*, *Mayflower*, *Vigilant* and *Defender*. 1930-1932: *Neponset*, *Columbia*, *Reliance* and *Resolute*, to be followed by *Enterprise* and *Ranger*.

Goodyear began construction of the world's largest hangar – the Air Dock – in 1928. It was 1,175ft long x 325ft wide x 197ft high, with a floor area of eight and a half acres. Underground there were storage tanks for helium. The Akron Air Dock is now listed as a National Historic Site.

No commercial rigid airships were built or operated in the United States, but some ambitious plans were laid. In 1921 the *American Investigation Corporation* was formed to examine the possibility of inaugurating scheduled air services with large rigid airships. Members of the group went on a fact-finding tour to France, Germany, Italy and the United Kingdom before announcing, in February 1922, the formation of the *General Air Service Corporation*, which would construct and operate the airships. The *New York Times* described it as 'a gigantic corporation for commercial navigation of the air in this country, through the establishment of regular lines over which will be operated huge dirigible airships of the modified Zeppelin type.' It was expected that two of these large airships would be operating between New York and Chicago by the summer of 1923, with services from a later date to the cities of the Pacific coast. Among those supporting the venture were the presidents of Hotchkiss, Westinghouse, the Mellon National Bank, Gulf Oil, Standard

Oil and Boeing. Two men prominent in promoting the scheme were Benedict Crowell (a former assistant secretary of war) and Franklin D. Roosevelt (a former assistant secretary of the navy).

The American Investigation Corporation signed a contract in 1922 with Dr Johann Schütte, president of the Schütte-Lanz Corporation, by which the Americans acquired the rights to the Schütte designs and construction methods. Johann Schütte was in the United States again in 1923, but by this time the American Investigation Corporation was in trouble – payments due to Schütte could not be made, and the Corporation became involved in a good deal of litigation. Before long it was bankrupt.

Military Airships

US Army

At the end of the First World War the United States Army acquired a handful of European dirigibles, including three *Submarine Scouts*, an *Astra-Torres* and a *Zodiac*.

In the early months of 1919 the Army Air Service set up a base for airships at Langley Field, on the coast of Virginia, and in the same year an airship shed was erected at Camp Owen Beirne, Fort Bliss, Texas; airships based here flew patrols along the US/Mexican border.

Roma

The US Army's semi-rigid *Roma* was built at the Italian Military Aircraft Factory and first flew on 16 September 1920. It was 412ft long x 82ft maximum diameter, with a capacity of 1,200,000 cubic feet. Powered by six 400hp Ansaldo engines, each driving a propeller, the airship could achieve 68mph. The cruising range was 5,300 miles. *Roma* was bought by the United States for $200,000 in February 1921, and next month it made a non-stop flight of 300 miles from Rome to Naples and back carrying fifty-two passengers, including the American ambassador and his wife with several American officers; lunch was served over Capri. The original plan was to fly the new acquisition to the United States, but the airship was dismantled and sent by ship, to be re-assembled at Langley Field.

The first ascent in America was on 15 November 1921. On a subsequent trip one of the propellers disintegrated, ripping open the envelope and gashing a gas container, but the airship came to earth safely.

The *Roma*, commanded by Major John Thornell, flew to Washington on 21 December. On the way there were frequent engine breakdowns because of the cold, and a strong headwind posed problems. The return flight to Langley was made without the use of two engines. It was decided to take out the Ansaldo engines and replace them with Liberty engines. (The Liberty engine was a standardised engine developed during the First World War, when thousands were produced by several manufacturers).

On 21 February 1922 the *Roma*, commanded by Captain Dale Mabry, went up for a flight over Langley Field to test the new engines. The airship became uncontrollable and went into a nose-dive, narrowly missing some buildings but hitting high tension electric cables. It burst into flames and exploded, killing thirty-four of the forty-six on board.

76 The US Army's semi-rigid *Roma* crashed at Langley Field on 21 February 1922. It hit high-tension wires and burst into flames. There were forty-six on board. Twelve survived.

TC-1

The *TC-1*, built by Airships Inc., was 196ft x 44ft, and 200,600 cubic feet. It was destroyed by fire at Wilbur Wright Field, Dayton, Ohio, in April 1923. The airship, moored to a mast, was caught by the wind and blown against a nearby steel pole. The two men on board leaped to safety, each breaking an ankle. *TC-2* was larger – 750,000 cubic feet – and designed to carry twelve aeroplanes in the interior of the airship.

TC-3 made 'hook-up' trials with a Sperry *Messenger* aeroplane in December 1924.

RS-1

Construction of the *RS-1* began at Akron towards the end of 1924, and the components were sent to Scott Field for assembly. This first American-built semi-rigid was 282ft x 70ft, 720,000 cubic feet, with four Liberty engines in two power gondolas. The enclosed control car was 35ft long and contained navigation equipment, sleeping accommodation, a radio compartment and a 'motion picture camera'. The bomb racks could carry 3,500lb, and machine-guns could be mounted on both sides of the control car. The ship was intended for training, patrol work and photographic reconnaissance.

By the early 1930s the army lighter-than-air establishment was twenty officers and 650 enlisted men. There were four non-rigids, of which the *TC-13* was the only one fully operational. At the same time, the US Army had nearly 1,000 aeroplanes.

In 1937 army airship activities were abandoned and *TC-13* and *TC-14* were transferred to the navy.

US Navy: Non-Rigids

Eight American-built (envelopes by Goodrich or Goodyear, gondolas by Curtiss) C class non-rigids were employed by the navy for training up to 1922. For four years from 1920, six D types were flown – these were modified C types, with a capacity of 190,000 cubic feet. There were also: one E type and one F type (both of 95,000 cubic feet). An H type was airborne in 1921: a small airship – 43,000 cubic feet, 40ft long – it flew six times; after one of these flights it escaped and was blown for some miles before being captured. After deflation it was housed at Rockaway, where it was destroyed in the hangar fire of 31 August 1921. *J-1* (210,600 cubic feet, 58ft long) was in commission for two years from August 1922; *J-3* was a modified army TC type which served at Lakehurst from October 1926, training crews for the large rigids *Los Angeles, Akron* and *Macon*. The airship was lost at sea while taking part in the search for survivors of the *Akron* in April 1933 – of the seven men on board, two died. *J-4* served as a trainer from November 1927 to March 1940. The Goodyear advertising and passenger blimp *Defender* (319,000 cubic feet) was bought by the navy in September 1935 and used for training until 8 June 1942, when it collided in mid-air with another blimp.

The Metalclad Airship

After seven years of research, led by Charles H. Fritsche and Ralph H. Upson, the Aircraft Development Corporation began construction of the *ZMC-2* at the Naval Air Station , Grosse Isle, near Detroit. The navy took delivery on 12 September 1929 at Lakehurst. The envelope of the experimental *ZMC-2* was made of 'Alclad' – duralumin sheets coated with aluminium. Flown by two men, the airship was 150ft long x 53ft diameter, with a capacity of 200,000 cubic feet. The two 300hp Wright Whirlwind engines produced a maximum speed of 70mph.

   ZMC-2 flew for over 2,000 hours in total before being deleted in 1941.

US Navy Rigid Airships

The Naval Appropriations Act of July 1919 included provision for the construction of one rigid airship (the *ZR-1*) and the purchase of another, which the navy decided would be the British *R38*, which was designated *ZR-2*.

ZR-1/Shenandoah

The *Shenandoah* was the first American-built rigid airship, and the first rigid to use helium as the lifting gas. Like the other large naval dirigibles, its planned role was to undertake long-range maritime reconnaissance. With a capacity of 2,115,000 cubic feet and 680ft long, the airship was assembled at Lakehurst from components manufactured by the Naval Aircraft Factory at Philadelphia. Six 300hp Packard engines produced a top speed of 60mph. Range was 5,000 miles, and the armament was six Lewis guns and eight 500lb bombs.

   The design of *Shenandoah* was based on the German naval Zeppelin *L49*, which had been captured almost undamaged at Bourbonne-Les-Bains in France in October 1917, modified in the light of British experience and information about Zeppelin *L72* (the reparations airship taken by France).

77 *Shenandoah* being assembled at Lakehurst.

Shenandoah's first ascent was on 4 September 1923 at Lakehurst; using only four of the six engines, and at only half speed, the airship was in the air for an hour. The captain was Commander F.R. McCrary, who was accompanied by R.D. Weyerbacher (responsible for construction at Lakehurst) and Anton Heinen, who had been a pilot for the Zeppelin Company. A week later the new ship was shown off over Philadelphia and New York City and, on 22 September, over Washington.

The summer of 1924 saw the *Shenandoah* taking part in naval exercises, and mooring trials with the *Patoka*, a vessel which had been adapted to become an airship tender, with a mooring-mast, storage for helium and petrol, accommodation for the airmen, and three seaplanes.

Shenandoah made the first flight by a rigid airship across North America in October 1924, trying out new mooring-masts at stops along the way. The *Shenandoah* was again involved in fleet exercises during the summer of 1925, and was towed whilst attached to *Patoka*'s mast. By the end of August the airship had been in commission for two years and had made fifty-seven flights totalling 540 hours.

At 3.00 p.m. on 2 September 1925, the *Shenandoah*, commanded by Zachary Lansdowne, lifted-off from Lakehurst for an extensive 'public relations' tour of the Midwest, setting course for Columbus, Ohio. Early next morning the airship was hit by thunderstorms and broke into three pieces with the bow and tail coming to earth twelve miles apart, near Caldwell, Noble County, Ohio. Of the forty-two men on board, thirteen died, including Commander Lansdowne.

The court of inquiry concluded that the airship's destruction was 'due primarily to large and unbalanced external aerodynamic forces arising from high velocity air currents.'

78 *Shenandoah* moored at the mast of the airship tender *Patoka*.

Colonel William (Billy) Mitchell had been a persistent advocate for an independent air arm, and after the *Shenandoah*'s demise he denounced the policy-makers and administrators: 'These accidents are the result of incompetency, criminal negligence, and almost treasonable administration by the War and Navy Departments.' As a result, President Coolidge set up an Air Board of Inquiry, and Mitchell resigned after a court-martial.

ZR-2

The *ZR-2* was the British *R38*, which came to grief during a test flight on 24 August 1921, killing forty-four men (see page 120).

ZR-3/Los Angeles

The *ZR-3* (Zeppelin *LZ126*) was built for the United States as a war reparations payment (see page 97). The delivery flight – of nearly eighty-one hours – from Friedrichshafen ended at Lakehurst on 15 October 1924, and as the Zeppelin passed over New York City:

79 *Los Angeles* in the hangar at Lakehurst. The airship was built at Friedrichshafen as Zeppelin *LZ126*. Its flight to Lakehurst, where it arrived on 15 October 1924, was commanded by Hugo Eckener.

> Thousands of work-bound halted in the streets, oblivious of all save the glittering shape drumming its way above. More thousands were encamped on the rooftops … others were summoned to see by their neighbours shouting across air shafts or courts … As the dirigible sailed up the river cheers went up from the crowded ferry-boats to aid the din of the harbor whistles (*New York Times*, 16 October 1924).

The commander, Hugo Eckener, and his colleagues were received at the White House by President Coolidge, and Eckener made public appearances in New York, Cleveland, Akron, Detroit, Chicago and Milwaukee.

The *Los Angeles* was accommodated in the big Lakehurst hangar. When the *Shenandoah* returned from its transcontinental voyage on 25 October its helium was transferred to the *Los Angeles* as there was not enough for both.

Los Angeles was used as a training and experimental ship, attracting huge crowds wherever it appeared, often at county fairs. In January 1925 the airship flew scientists to observe the total eclipse of the sun, and four months later it cruised the Caribbean, spending time at *Patoka*'s mast. *Saratoga*, the navy's first fast aircraft carrier, came into service in January 1928 – its first aircraft landed on 11 January and on the 27th Lieutenant-Commander Rosendahl in *Los Angeles* followed suit, taking on stores and fuel.

The *Los Angeles* also took part in experiments with aeroplanes and on 3 July 1929, a Vought UO-1 biplane, piloted by Lieutenant A.W. Gorton, hooked on to a trapeze and then disengaged at 2,500ft while the airship was travelling at 48knots.

The *Los Angeles* was decommissioned at the end of June 1932, as an economy measure. It was brought back into service for a short period after the crash of the *Akron* but it was soon mothballed, before being deleted in 1939.

ZRS-4/Akron

The navy's rigid airships *Akron* and *Macon* were built by the Goodyear-Zeppelin Corporation as flying aircraft-carriers. The idea was to use small aeroplanes to extend the

80 A Curtiss F9C Sparrowhawk in *Akron*'s hangar – four such aircraft could be fitted into a space measuring 75ft x 50ft.

area of reconnaissance, and for defence of the airship. Each ship could carry four aeroplanes within the hull, in a space 75ft x 50ft. The airships had a capacity of 6,500,000 cubic feet and were 758ft long x 133ft diameter. Driven by 560hp Maybach engines (eight in *Akron*, six in *Macon*) their top speed was over 80mph.

Akron first flew on 23 September 1931, was delivered to the US Navy at Lakehurst a month later, and took part in fleet exercises in January 1932.

On 3 May 1932 aeroplanes were flown to the trapeze for the first time by Lieutenants D.H. Harrigan and H.L. Young. Five days later the *Akron* set off for a month's stay at Sunnyvale, California. Flying down the east coast and then over Georgia, Texas and Arizona the airship arrived at Camp Kearny, near San Diego, on 11 May. Two men of the ground crew were killed in an accident during the first attempt at mooring.

The airship made many appearances over towns in California, and scouted for the Green Force in exercises over the Pacific. Leaving Sunnyvale on 11 June 1932, the *Akron* took four days to arrive at Lakehurst. Trials with the aeroplane trapeze continued through the summer and in the autumn reconnaissance patrols were made over the Atlantic by the *Akron* and her aircraft.

Commander Frank C. McCord took charge of the airship in January 1933, and soon started on a cruise to Cuba, carrying a group inspecting possible airship bases. 3 March was the inauguration day of President Franklin D. Roosevelt, at which *Akron* made a stately appearance. Leaving Lakehurst on 11 March the airship went to Panama, so that another potential base could be examined. On the return leg a stop was made at the naval reserve training base at Opa-Locka, Florida, where the crew practiced firing the airship's guns.

81 *Macon* over New York City. The airship was first airborne in June 1933 and was to be lost off the coast of California in February 1935.

The *Akron*'s next task was a flight along the New England coast, to provide practice for radio direction-finding stations. The chief of the Bureau of Aeronautics, Admiral Moffett, was on board. Leaving Lakehurst late on 3 April 1933 the airship ran into a storm during which, in the early hours of 4 April, the rudder cables were ripped away. *Akron* crashed into the sea. Seventy-three died and only three survived, rescued by a German ship.

President Roosevelt's message said:

> The loss of the *Akron* with its crew of gallant officers and men is a national disaster. I grieve with the Nation and especially with the wives and families of the men who were lost. Ships can be replaced, but the Nation can ill afford to lose such men as Rear Admiral William A. Moffett and his shipmates who died with him upholding to the end the finest traditions of the United States Navy.

ZRS-5 / Macon

Three weeks before the loss of the *Akron*, the new rigid airship had been named *Macon* by the wife of Admiral Moffett. Just over a fortnight after the *Akron* disaster, *Macon* made its first flight. On 23/24 June 1933, captained by Commander Alger H. Dresel, it was delivered to Lakehurst. On board were Admiral E.J. King, Paul W. Litchfield (president of Goodyear) and the company's chief engineer, Dr Karl Arnstein.

The next three months were occupied with practising flying aeroplanes to and from the airship, before departing for Moffett Field (formerly Sunnyvale, but renamed from 1 September) on 12 October 1933. From its new base *Macon* took part in exercises over the Pacific, sending off its aircraft on scouting missions.

The *Macon* was lost on 12 February 1935, when it came down into the sea near Point Sur lighthouse, California. Rubber lifeboats were launched, and seventy-eight of the eighty people on board were rescued.

A naval board of inquiry was convened in San Francisco. Lieutenant Calvin Bolster (the 'repairs officer' of the *Macon*) gave his view that the airship lost height because of a failure of the upper fin. 'The failure of the fin involved failure of the fin structure and the structure of the ship where the fin was supported.' During a recent flight over Texas, the airship had met heavy turbulence and had dropped rapidly, causing damage to a girder supporting the forward fins. After inspection at Moffett Field it was decided that the girder's supporting fins should be strengthened, but the top fin's girders had not been modified before *Macon*'s last flight. Lieutenant Bolster stated that the Bureau of Aeronautics had ordered that the airship should fly.

In his summing up the judge advocate concluded that the accident had been caused by a design fault – a gust of wind hit the airship's upper fin, putting under stress the forward part and four bolts at the base of one of the frames. This led to a girder giving way and puncturing gas cells, which caused the tail of the *Macon* to drop into the sea.

The day after the loss the chairman of the Naval Affairs Committee of the House of Representatives, Carl Vinson, said that this might prove to be the death-knell of the navy's experiment with airships. President Roosevelt stated that the administration did not intend to fund another airship 'at the present time'.

V

THE SECOND WORLD WAR AND AFTER

Britain declared war on Germany on 3 September 1939. Although air power was to play a hugely significant role in the war, there were no European dirigibles. The Soviet Union had one – the *W12* – which was used for parachute training. The United States, on the other hand, deployed a large number.

UNITED STATES NAVY AIRSHIPS

Japanese carrier-borne aircraft attacked the US Pacific Fleet at Pearl Harbor on 7 December 1941, and four days later Germany declared war on the United States. At this time the US Navy's airships, all non-rigid, were:

G class – *G1* was the Goodyear advertising blimp *Defender* which had been bought by the navy in 1935. On 8 June 1942 it collided with *L2* on a night flight, killing twelve people, including civilian scientists.
K class – *K2, K3, K4* and *K5*. Built from 1938 onwards and used for patrolling.
L class – *L1, L2* and *L3*. Small training craft.
TC class – *TC13* and *TC14* had been taken over by the army in 1937.

By early 1942 the Goodyear blimps *Resolute, Enterprise, Reliance, Rainbow* and *Ranger* had been acquired by the navy and designated *L4* to *L8*. On 16 August Lieutenant Cody and Ensign Adams took off in *L8* for a patrol flight off San Francisco. The airship came down inland, but Cody and Adams were never found. The *L8* was repaired and saw out the rest of the war.

Airships Built During the War

G class: *G2* to *G5* were in service by late 1943; *G6* to *G8* by early 1944. These seven blimps were used as trainers, mostly at Lakehurst and Moffett Field.

L class: Fourteen more L class blimps were ordered: *L9* to *L12* were assembled at Moffett Field and were flying by April 1943. By the end of the year *L13* to *L22* had been delivered from Goodyear. Used for training, they were 148ft long with a capacity of 123,000 cubic feet, and a crew of two.

82 A K class blimp escorting a convoy. During the Second World War most of the US Navy's airships were of this type. 252ft long, they were flown by a crew of eight to ten.

M class: Four were built by Goodyear. Intended for anti-submarine warfare, they were nearly 290ft long, driven by two 500hp Pratt & Whitney engines. Their capacity was 625,000 cubic feet.

K class: This type made up the bulk of the US airship fleet – Goodyear built 133 of them between 1942 and 1945. 252ft long, with a capacity of 425,000 cubic feet, they were manned by a crew of eight to ten. With two 425hp Pratt & Whitney engines the airships had a top speed of over 70mph and could stay aloft for twenty-four hours. The 40ft gondola contained radar and other electronic equipment, and there were four depth charges and a Browning machine-gun. For mooring a triangular, 40ft high, moveable mast could be used, and the airship could be walked into the hangar still attached to the mast.

During the Second World War the US Navy operated the largest ever airship fleet. Its initial organisation was:

Fleet Airship Wing One flew from Lakehurst (New Jersey), Glynco (Georgia), Weeksville (North Carolina), South Weymouth (Massachusetts), Brunswick and Bar Harbour (Maine), Yarmouth (Nova Scotia) and Argentia (Newfoundland).

Fleet Airship Wing Two, from its HQ at Richmond (Florida), covered the Gulf of Mexico and the northern Caribbean.

83 US Navy blimp *N-1*, launched by Goodyear in 1951, became *ZPG-1* in 1954. It was to be followed by a series of large non-rigid airships of over 1,000,000 cubic feet capacity, which had been developed for early-warning duties and anti-submarine warfare.

Fleet Airship Wing Three controlled units at Santa Anna, Moffett Field and Tillamook, Oregon.

Fleet Airship Wing Four operated along the coast of Brazil.

Fleet Airship Wing Five: Trinidad, British Guiana and Dutch Guiana.

Only one airship was lost to enemy action. On the night of 18/19 July 1943 *K74*, patrolling off the coast of Florida, attacked the German submarine *U-134* which returned fire, bringing down the blimp. One man died in the sea but the nine survivors were picked up by the destroyer USS *Dahlgren*, although Lieutenant Grills was in the water for nineteen hours before being rescued. The U-boat was sunk a month later, with all hands, in the Bay of Biscay.

The airships *K123* and *K130* became the first non-rigids to cross the Atlantic. On 28 May 1944 they flew from the Naval Air Station at South Weymouth to Argentia, Newfoundland, reaching the Azores on the 31st and Port Lyautey, Morocco, on 1 June. In another month all six of Blimp Squadron 14's craft were in Morocco, to be employed on patrolling the Straits of Gibraltar, looking for mines and submarines, and escorting convoys.

Post-War

The war in Europe ended on 5 May 1945 and in the Pacific on 15 August 1945. In the immediate post-war period the Soviet Union flew the *W12 bis*, usually for propaganda purposes and over military parades. There was also an airship of the *Pobeida* class, which was used for mine-spotting until it crashed in January 1947.

The US Naval Air Service was reduced to two airship squadrons, operating in an 'early warning' role along the Atlantic coast and in the Caribbean. In the early 1950s two more squadrons were formed, along with an Airship Development Squadron (disbanded in 1957) at Key West. An Airship Airborne Early Warning Squadron was in existence from January 1958 to October 1961.

K class

A number of K class ships continued in commission, now being designated the *ZKP* class. Fifteen K ships were rebuilt by Goodyear with a capacity of 527,000 cubic feet, and as *ZSG* types they were employed until 1959. (From 1954 navy airships had the builder's initial included in the type designation: thus *ZSG* indicated a Goodyear ship).

Another development was the *ZSG2G1* type (527,000 cubic feet) with two 800hp Curtiss Wright engines. These airships undertook very long anti-submarine missions.

N class

ZPN-1 became *ZPG-1* in 1954. It was the forerunner of a series of large airships, all built by Goodyear, for early warning and anti-submarine missions.

ZPG-2. Twelve of these airships came into service from 1955. They were 343ft long x 75ft maximum diameter, with a capacity of 1,100,000 cubic feet. Powered by two 800hp Wright Cyclone engines, the maximum speed was nearly 90mph. The gondola was 83ft long and 11ft wide, on two levels: the upper part contained the crew's quarters, the lower part was for controlling the ship.

In May 1954 a *ZPG-2*, captained by Commander Henry Eppes, stayed airborne for 200 hours and six minutes, breaking the record of 170.3 hours set by an M type in 1947. Commander Eppes took his airship from Lakehurst to Nova Scotia, Bermuda, Nassau, the Gulf of Mexico and Key West.

Another endurance flight was made in 1957, in a *ZPG-2* captained by Commander Jack R. Hunt – a voyage which lasted for over eleven days: across the Atlantic (the first non-stop crossing by a non-rigid airship) to Portugal, the Cape Verde Islands, Puerto Rico and Key West. The blimp had flown 9,448 miles.

In 1958 a *ZPG-2* flew to the Arctic and delivered stores to a research station.

ZPG-2W. This variant had two radar domes: one on the top of the envelope and the other inside. Manned by a crew of twenty-one, it was used to fill gaps in the United States' early warning network.

ZPG-3W. There were four of these – the largest non-rigid airships ever built, with a capacity of 1,516,000 cubic feet. The first flew in July 1958.

Two years later a *ZPG-3W* crashed suddenly into the Atlantic off New Jersey with the loss of three of the twenty-one men on board. *The Times* (8 July 1960) reported the views of 'retired Vice-Admiral Rosendahl, America's greatest expert in lighter-than-air transport:

> Who declared in Washington today that the loss of the blimp was 'undoubtedly related to the questionable wisdom of building such large airships on the non-compartmented or blimp principle. This, in turn,' he said 'stems from the Navy's continued blind refusal to properly evaluate, admit and benefit from the rigid airship lessons of the past.'

In 1962 the US Navy ceased all airship operations.

In 2005 the US Navy Air Systems Command acquired an *A-150* (built by the American Blimp Corporation) for a series of evaluation flights from the Naval Air Station at Patuxent River, Maryland. In the following year a naval airship flew from Lakehurst (now a naval air engineering station) for the first time in nearly forty-four years when an *A-170*, bought from the American Blimp Company, began trials as a platform for the development of electronic systems.

84 A *Zeppelin NT* began pleasure flights over Lake Constance in July 2001. The fourth *Zeppelin NT* flew in May 2008. Able to carry twelve passengers, it was based at Moffett Field, California.

COMMERCIAL AIRSHIPS

Advertising on airships had been there from the early days – in 1902 the first British airship advertised Mellin's baby foods, and in 1905 Baldwin's dirigible promoted 'Gelatine' at Portland, Oregon. In the period after the Second World War airships reverted to this commercial role, with advertisements placed on hired blimps – a practice which made it appear that there were many different craft, but one blimp could be flown under several names.

An example of this was the German *Trumpf III*, which first flew in 1958. With a capacity of 158,900 cubic feet, the blimp was 160ft long x 43ft maximum diameter. (This was not the first airship promoting Trumpf chocolate: two of the Parseval-Naatz type – 60,000 cubic feet – did the same in the late twenties and early thirties.) From 1970 the *Trumpf III* became the *Braun Sixtant* – named after an electric razor – and was operated from Mannheim by WDL (Westdeutsche Luftwerbung – West German Aerial Advertising). WDL went on to build five more blimps at Essen-Mülheim: two WDL-1 types in 1972 (184ft x 47ft, 216,000 cubic feet, with two crew and seven passengers) and, between 1988 and 1990, three others which were larger versions of the WDL-1. Computer-generated signs were installed for display after dark. As well as making advertising flights, WDL blimps were hired for television and film work, and for surveillance.

Another German airship, the prototype *Zeppelin NT* (290,000 cubic feet; 246ft long), made its first flight in September 1997. In 2005 the *Zeppelin NT* prototype – chartered for two years by De Beers – went prospecting for diamonds in Botswana.

The first production airship built by Zeppelin Luftschifftechnik began carrying fare-paying passengers on pleasure flights from Friedrichshafen in July 2001. It was operated by a subsidiary of Zeppelin Luftschifftechnik: Deutsche Zeppelin Reederei – a familiar name from the 1930s. This airship was sold to Japan in 2004, to fly under the name *Yokuso Japan*. The *Zeppelin NT* incorporated a basic system of rigid girders, combined with a pressurised envelope. There were three 200hp Lycoming engines, which could swivel up to 120 degrees. Computer-aided control systems were installed.

The third *Zeppelin NT* took to the air in February 2003 and the fourth on 21 May 2008 – the latter (246ft long, able to carry twelve passengers) was bought by Airship Ventures Inc. to be based at Moffett Field, California.

In Britain, airships were again built at Cardington, but these were small, non-rigid advertising craft. The *AD500*, constructed by Airship Industries, made its first flight in February 1979. It was 171ft long x 40ft diameter, with a capacity of 182,000 cubic feet. With a crew of two, it could carry eight passengers. These blimps were driven by two 200hp Porsche engines installed in the fibreglass gondola and driving ducted fans which could be tilted to make the craft ascend or descend.

The *AD500* became known as *Skyship 500–01*. *Skyship 500–02* followed in September 1981, emulating early British airships with a publicity flight over London in April 1982. Eight months later the blimp spent a week in Paris, making daily trips between the Charles de Gaulle and Orly airports. *500–03* was based at Weeksville, North Carolina, and used for pilot training and demonstration flights for the US Navy, Coast Guard and Westinghouse. *500–04* was employed at the Los Angeles Olympic Games, *500–05* was flown by Nikko Trading in Japan.

Ten of the *Skyship 600* series were constructed by Airship Industries, flying from March 1984. They were an enlarged version of the *500*, with a capacity of 234,000 cubic feet, a length of 194ft, and two 230hp Porsche engines. Blimps of the *600* series flew in Australia, Japan, Korea and the United States.

The company worked with the Westinghouse Defense Group to design and build the *Sentinel 1000* airship. The gondola and turbo-charged engines were the same as in the 600 series, but the envelope was enlarged to a capacity of 353,140 cubic feet. The *1000* was built as a preliminary to the *Sentinel 5000* for the US Navy, which gave it the designation of *YEZ-2A*. The *New York Times* (10 January 1989) described the new airship: 'A quarter century after the United States Navy consigned its last dirigible airship to the scrap heap of antiquated weaponry a gigantic new blimp is taking shape to defend America against cruise missiles, drug smugglers and a host of modern threats.' When Airship Industries went out of business, in September 1990, Westinghouse continued the development of the *Sentinel*, but it was to be destroyed by fire in 1995, in its hangar at Weeksville, North Carolina.

With the demise of Airship Industries, Westinghouse acquired the British firm's Skyship designs. These passed to Global Skyship Industries and their associate company Airship Management Services (based in Greenwich, Connecticut) which operated Skyships.

The first thermal airship, designed and built by Cameron Balloons Ltd, made its maiden flight at Wantage on 4 January 1974. A thermal airship is a balloon made in the shape of an airship, and inflated with hot air rather than helium. Propane burners heat the air, and an engine drives the craft along at no more than 15mph, carrying a pilot and a passenger, but only in light winds and for short distances. Thermal airships have been built in Britain by Cameron Balloons, Thunder and Colt, and by Lindstrand Industries. They usually have a capacity of between 110,000 and 120,000 cubic feet, and can be packed up and transported on a trailer.

Thunder and Colt built six small helium airships at their factory near Oswestry in Shropshire between 1987 and 1992. The *GA-42,* which first flew in July 1988, was 92ft long x 30ft diameter, with a capacity of 42,000 cubic feet. The 100hp engine drove the two-seater at speeds of up to 40mph. The rights to the *GA-42* were bought by the American Blimp Company at the end of 1994, when Thunder and Colt merged with Cameron Balloons. Production of Thunder and Colt balloons and hot-air airships moved to the Cameron factory at Bristol.

Goodyear has generally operated three advertising blimps in America, with names such as *America, Columbia, Eagle, Enterprise, Mayflower, Spirit of Akron, Spirit of America, Spirit of Goodyear* and *Spirit of Innovation.* There were, usually, never more than three in commission at the same time. In 2008 the three were: *Spirit of America,* based at Carson, California; *Spirit of Goodyear,* based at Akron, Ohio; and *Spirit of Innovation,* at Pompano Beach, Florida. Each was capable of carrying six passengers.

Components of the Goodyear blimp *Europa* were flown from Akron to Cardington for assembly. It was 192ft long x 46ft diameter, with a capacity of 202,700 cubic feet and two 210hp engines. The first flight was made, at Cardington, on 8 March 1972. Equipped with a 'night sign' for after-dark advertising, *Europa* was operated from Capena, near Rome, and apart from advertising was used for television coverage of public events, and for wildlife filming. In 1986 the *Europa* was returned to the United States.

Goodyear's *GZ-22* made its first flight in 1987 – it was 205ft long, driven by turbo-jet engines, and controlled by fly-by-wire technology. The airship was decommissioned in 1999.

The American Blimp Corporation was founded in 1987. A prototype Lightship, the *A-50,* was followed by the production of the *A-60,* built at Hillsboro, Oregon – four were bought by Virgin Airships. In 1991 the *A-60* was enlarged to become the *A-60+,* with a capacity of 68,000 cubic feet and a length of 135ft. It could carry a maximum of four passengers. The envelope was translucent and could be illuminated from the inside for night-time display.

85 *Spirit of Europe II* arrived in Europe in 1998. It was an *A60+* Lightship, owned by the UK Lightship Group. It appeared at events such as football matches, motor races and tennis tournaments.

From 1993 blimps were operated by Lightship America, a subsidiary of the American Blimp Corporation. Two years later the Lightship Group was set up as a joint venture of Lightship America and Virgin Airships, which controlled the activities of seven *A-60+* Lightships from offices at Telford (UK) and Orlando (Florida). By 2002 Virgin Airships had withdrawn from the partnership, leaving ABC in control of the Lightship Group, operating sixteen airships.

An *A-60+* was employed as a 'mineseeker' in Kosovo in October and November 2000. It was flown from Britain and then used ground-penetrating radar to locate and survey thirty minefields, collecting sixty hours of videotape and 500 digital images.

In 1997 the first *A-150* type was built for the Sanyo North America Corporation, and in May 2004 the first *A-170* (170,000 cubic feet) appeared. Two years later an *A-170* was produced with a 70ft x 30ft LED screen, capable of showing live television and slide shows. A military version of the *A-170* was ordered by the US Navy.

Airship Management Services of Greenwich, Connecticut, operates Skyships. The *500HL* has a capacity of 235,000 cubic feet, is 194ft long, and can carry nine passengers. The *Skyship 600* is 200ft long, has a capacity of 254,000 cubic feet, and can accommodate twelve passengers. In November 2006 a *Skyship 600* with the name *Spirit of Dubai* set off from Cardington. The purpose of the flight was to promote a large artificial island built at Dubai, and it was planned to visit London, Paris, Rome and Cairo. The airship arrived at Crete in January 2007, but could not obtain permission to fly over Egypt and therefore made for Friedrichshafen. It was there for about five months before going to Poland to advertise a local company.

Worldwide Aeros Corporation was founded by Ukrainian immigrant Igor Pasternak. Based in California, it manufactures blimps at Montebello and flies them from San Bernadino. The range includes the *Aeros-40A* (122ft long), *Aeros-40B Sky Dragon* (143ft long, 88,570 cubic feet), *Aeros-40C* (197ft, 247,200 cubic feet, thirteen passengers) and *Aeros-50* (977ft, 26,246 cubic feet).

The airships flying in the twenty-first century are used in much the same way as those of a century ago: for advertising and for observation. Conveying passengers is not a major activity – with the exception of the *Zeppelin NT*, which provides short sight-seeing trips – but airship flights never were for the masses, they were a perquisite of the wealthy. Advertisers hiring a blimp today display their logo on the envelope just as in the early days. One development is that technology now enables night-signs to be displayed after dark, although it should be remembered that this kind of advertising is not new – it was first tried out on a Parseval over Berlin in 1912.

The use of balloons for observation, now often called 'surveillance', began late in the eighteenth century and was continued throughout the nineteenth. The practice was developed further by the use of balloons, kites and blimps during the First World War, and then by the large rigid airships. Today surveillance is often by electronic means, and a small non-rigid airship is likely to be employed as a stable platform for a camera to convey and record images of what is happening on the ground.

What of the future? Airships have less impact on the environment than other types of flying machines: they are quiet, manoeuvrable, use less fuel, and need no long runway. An airship can hover or fly slowly. On the other hand, being slow can also be a disadvantage, as can the fact that, at the present time, an airship can carry few passengers, and is likely to be put in jeopardy by strong winds.

Small airships will continue to be favoured by advertisers, and to be deployed for some kinds of surveillance: military as well as civil, perhaps unmanned. Other developments may include their use for tourism, disaster relief, and for moving heavy cargoes. It may be that the future lies with a hybrid design – combining the lighter-than-air properties of an airship with the aerodynamic qualities of a fixed-wing aircraft.

AIRSHIP TIMELINE

21 November 1783: First manned flight: J.F. Pilâtre de Rozier and the marquis d'Arlandes, in a hot-air balloon.

1 December 1783: First flight in a hydrogen-filled balloon: J.A.C. Charles and Nicolas Robert.

27 August 1784: First balloon flight in Scotland: James Tytler.

15 September 1784: First balloon flight in England: Vincenzo Lunardi.

4 October 1784: First English aviator: James Sadler.

7 January 1785: First flight across the English Channel: J-P. Blanchard and John Jeffries.

9 January 1793: First untethered balloon flight in the United States: J.P. Blanchard.

1794: Balloon first used for military observation.

19 July 1821: First use of coal gas to fill a balloon: Charles Green, London.

9 September 1830: First American aeronaut – balloon flight from New York City to Perth Amboy, New Jersey: Charles Ferson Durant.

24 September 1852: Henri Giffard's steam-powered airship, Paris.

12 June 1878: Charles Francis Ritchel's man-powered dirigible at Hartford, Connecticut.

8 October 1883: The Tissandier brothers' airship, driven by an electric motor, Paris.

9 August 1884: Airship *La France*, with an electric motor, flies for five miles and returns to starting point: Arthur Krebs and Charles Renard.

1895: Internal combustion engine installed in an airship: Friedrich Hermann Wölfert.

1897: Experiments with a man-powered dirigible in Russia by Konstantin Danielevski.

November 1897: David Schwarz's aluminium airship, Berlin.

2 July 1900: Count Zeppelin's first airship flies at Lake Constance.

19 October 1901: Santos Dumont wins the Deutsch de la Meurthe prize by flying round the Eiffel Tower.

1902: The first British dirigible: Spencer Brothers.

1902: The first Lebaudy airship.

29 July 1904: The first American dirigible: Thomas Scott Baldwin's *California Arrow*.

1905: *Italia* flies at Schio, Italy.

June 1905: *Willows No.1* flies at Cardiff.

July 1905: First airship flight over New York City: A. Roy Knabenshue.

28 May 1906: First flight of August von Parseval's airship, Berlin.

August 1906: First airship flight over Washington D.C: Lincoln Beachey.

29 July 1907: Experimental airship of Hans Gross and Nikolaus Basenach, Berlin.

2 September 1907: Walter Wellman attempts to fly from Spitzbergen to the North Pole in airship *America*.

10 September 1907: First British Army airship, *Nulli Secundus*.

1 July 1908: Zeppelin *LZ4* makes twelve-hour non-stop flight.

August 1908: Destruction of *LZ4* at Echterdingen results in wave of popular support for Count Zeppelin.

1908: First US Army airship: *SC-1*

August 1909: Walter Wellman makes another attempt to fly to the North Pole.

November 1909: DELAG airline founded with headquarters at Frankfürt am Main.

6/7 August 1910: Ernest Willows makes night flight from Cardiff to London in *Willows No.2*.

15 October 1910: *Clément-Bayard II* makes first airship flight from France to Britain.

4 November 1910: Ernest Willows and Frank Goodden make the first airship flight from England to France.

September 1911: British rigid airship *Mayfly* breaks in two on emerging from shed.

1911–12: Italians use airships in war in north Africa.

18 October 1913: Zeppelin *LZ18* explodes at Berlin, killing all twenty-eight on board.

3 August 1914: Germany declares war on France.

5/6 August 1914: German airship bombs Liège.

August 1914: Four German airships are lost in the first month of the war.

19/20 January 1915: First airship raid on Britain.

31 May 1915: London bombed by German Army airship *LZ38*.

2/3 September 1916: Sixteen German airships attack Britain in the biggest airship raid of the war.

27 November 1916: Flight of first British rigid airship.

December 1916: US Navy's first blimp, *DN-1*.

6 April 1917: United States enters First World War.

November 1917: The Zeppelin 'Africa Ship' covers 4,340 miles in ninety-five hours, non-stop.

11 November 1918: Armistice.

July 1919: British *R34* makes first airship flight across the Atlantic.

21 July 1919: Goodyear *Wingfoot Express* crashes on to a bank building in Chicago, killing eight and injuring twenty-seven.

24 August 1921: Crash of airship *R38/ZR-2* off Hull, killing forty-four people.

21 February 1922: Thirty-four die when *Roma* crashes at Langley Field.

21 December 1923: French rigid airship *Dixmude* explodes over the Mediterranean, killing fifty people.

May 1924: British government's Imperial Airship Scheme announced.

October 1924: *Los Angeles*, built by Zeppelin, flies from Friedrichshafen to New York.

3 September 1925: Thirteen die in crash of *Shenandoah* in Ohio.

May 1926: *Norge* flies from Spitzbergen to Alaska over the North Pole.

October 1928: *Graf Zeppelin* makes first transatlantic passenger flight.

1929: *Graf Zeppelin* flies around the world.

July 1930: British *R100* flies from Cardington to Montreal and back.

October 1930: British *R101* on its way to India crashes in northern France, killing forty-eight.

1930: *Graf Zeppelin* flies to South America.

1931: *Graf Zeppelin* flies to the Arctic.

1932: Scheduled Zeppelin airship services to South America begin.

4 April 1933: Seventy-three people die when the US Navy's *Akron* crashes into the sea.

12 February 1935: US Navy's *Macon* forced down on the sea off the coast of California. Two people die.

May 1936: *Hindenburg*'s first flight to United States.

6 May 1937: *Hindenburg*, approaching the mooring-mast at Lakehurst, is destroyed by fire, killing thirty-five people.

1941–1945: US deploys large fleet of blimps in the Second World War.

1945–Present: Use of small blimps for advertising and surveillance.

SOURCES AND BIBLIOGRAPHY

Abbot, Patrick, *Airship: The Story of the First East-West Crossing of the Atlantic by Air* (Adams and Dart, 1973)

Abbot, Patrick, *Airship: The Story of the R34* (Brewin Books, 1994)

Baker, Anne Pimlott (2004), 'Cox', (Harold) Roxbee, Baron Kings Norton (1902 – 1997)' *Oxford Dictionary of National Biography*

Brew, Alec, *Boulton Paul Aircraft since 1915* (Brasseys, 1993)

Brooks, Peter W., *Historic Airships* (Hugh Evelyn, 1973)

Burney, Charles Dennistoun, *The World, the Air, and the Future* (Alfred A. Knopf, 1929)

Capelotti, P.J; Van Dyk, H; Caillez, J.C. (2007) Strange interlude at Virgohamna, Danskøya, Svalbard, 1906: the 'merkelig mann,' the engineer and the spy *Polar Research* 26 (1), 64–75

Duggan, John and Meyer, Henry Cord (2001) *Airships in International Affairs, 1891 – 1940* (Palgrave)

Duggan, John, *The Siemens-Schuckert Airship* (Ickenham: Zeppelin Study Group, 2002)

Ege, Lennart, *Balloons and Airships 1783 – 1973* (Blandford, 1973)

Fegan, Thomas, *The 'Baby Killers'. German Air Raids on Britain in the First World War* (Leo Cooper, 2002)

Foss, Clive, Russia's romance with the airship (*History Today*, Dec. 1997, 10–16)

Franks, Norman; Bailey, Frank; Duiven, Rick, *Casualties of the German Air Service 1914 – 1920* (Grub Street, 1999)

Gilbert, Martin, *Winston S. Churchill*, Vol.V 1922 – 1939 (Heinemann, 1976)

Gillispie, Charles Coulson, *The Montgolfier Brothers and the Invention of Aviation 1783 – 1784* (Princeton University Press, 1983)

Grant, R.G., *Flight: 100 Years of Aviation* (Dorling Kindersley, 2004)

Grossnick, Roy A. (Ed), *Kite Balloons to Airships: The Navy's Lighter-than-Air Experience* (Washington: Government Printing Office)

Guillemin, Jack and Nicodème, Philippe, *Dans le Ciel de Maubeuge 1794 – 1920. L'extrordinaire aventure des ballons et des dirigeables* (2006)

Higham, Robin, *The British Rigid Airship 1908 – 1931. A Study in Weapons Policy* (G.T. Foulis, 1961)

Higham, Robin; Greenwood, John T.; Hardesty, Von (Eds) *Russian Aviation and Air Power in the Twentieth Century* (Frank Cass, 1998)

Higham, Robin Brancker, Sir William Sefton (1877–1930), *Oxford Dictionary of National Biography* (OUP, 2004)

Hildebrandt, A., *Airships Past and Present* (1908)

Hirschel, E.H; Prem, H: Madelung, G., *Aeronautical Research in Germany. From Lilienthal until Today* (Springer, 2004)

Jones, H.A., revised by Curthoys, M.C., Scott, George Herbert (1888 – 1930), *Oxford Dictionary of National Biography* (2004)

Layman, R.D., *Naval Aviation in the First World War. Its Impact and Influence* (Chatham, 1996)

Maurer, M., *Aviation in the US Army* (Washington: Office of Air Force History, 1987)

Mowforth, Edwin, *An Introduction to the Airship* (3rd Edition 2006, London: The Airship Association)

Mowthorpe, Ces, *Battlebags: British Airships of the First World War: An Illustrated History* (Allan Sutton, 1995)

Neumann, Paul, *The German Air Force in the Great War* (Naval and Military Press, 1920)

Onslow, rev. Higham, Robin, Thomson, Christopher Birdwood, Baron Thomson (1875–1930), *Oxford Dictionary of National Biography* (OUP, 2004)

Paice, Edward, *Tip and Run: The Untold Tragedy of the First World War in Africa* (Weidenfeld, 2007)

Palmer, Scott W., *Dictatorship of the Air: Aviation Culture and the Fate of Modern Russia* (Cambridge University Press, 2006)

Pesce, Giuseppe, *The Italian Airships. English photographic edition* (Mucchi Editore, 1983)

Raleigh, Walter, *The War in the Air: Being the story of the part played by the Royal Air Force. Volume I*, (1969 Edition: Hamish Hamilton, 1922)

Report of the R101 Inquiry (HMSO 1931 Cmd 3825)

Robinson, Douglas H., *The Zeppelin in Combat: A History of the German Naval Airship Division, 1912 – 1918* (G.T. Foulis, 1971)

Rolt, L.T.C., *The Aeronauts: a history of ballooning, 1783 – 1903* (1966)

Ryan, A.P. rev by Sayoni Basu, Norway, Nevil Shute (1899–1960), *Oxford Dictionary of National Biography* (2004)

Shute, Nevil, *Slide Rule* (House of Stratus, 2000)

Syon, Guillaume de, *Zeppelin! Germany and the Airship, 1900 – 1939* (Johns Hopkins University Press, 2002)

Topping, Dale, *When Giants Roamed the Sky: Karl Arnstein and the rise of airships from Zeppelin to Goodyear* (University of Akron Press, 2001)

Ventry, Lord and Kolesnik, Eugene, *Jane's Pocket Book of Airships* (Macmillan, 1976)

Walker, Percy B., *Early Aviation at Farnborough. The History of the Royal Aircraft Establishment. Volume I – Balloons, Kites and Airships* (Macdonald, 1971).

Walker, Percy B., *Early Aviation at Farnborough. The history of the Royal Aircraft Establishment. Volume II – The First Aeroplanes* (Macdonald)

Walmsley, Nick le N., *'Dixmude': The Airship and her Commander from Contemporary Sources* (Walmsley for the Airship Heritage Trust, 1999)

Ward, B. R., *Manual of Miltary Ballooning* (Rediscovery Books, 1896. 2006 reproduction)

Wellman, W., *The aerial age* (Keller, 1911)

Whale, George, *British Airships, Past, Present and Future* (John Lane, 1919)

INDEX